Front-Page Scotland

This book provides a varied, thorough and informative analysis of how newspapers covered the 2014 Scottish independence referendum in its critical final months.

Providing a wealth of new observations, the book engages with the key themes and issues presented by a variety of newspaper outlets. These main observations include: a major focus on the economic aspects of the debate; persistent concerns regarding an independent Scotland's prospects on the world stage, both militarily and strategically; the re-emergence of Gordon Brown as a political heavyweight; and a myopic focus on Alex Salmond, who would come to be framed as personally synonymous with the abstract concept of Scottish independence.

The book will be the first point of contact for readers interested in the subject, providing an overview which is meticulously researched, authoritative and engaging, offering broader insights in the areas of journalism, political communication and media studies.

David Patrick is a Senior Researcher in the International Studies Group at the University of the Free State, Bloemfontein, South Africa.

Routledge Focus on Journalism Studies

For more information about this series, please visit: https://www.routledge.com

Front-Page Scotland

Newspapers and the Scottish
Independence Referendum

David Patrick

LONDON AND NEW YORK

First published 2022
by Routledge
2 Park Square, Milton Park, Abingdon, Oxon OX14 4RN

and by Routledge
605 Third Avenue, New York, NY 10158

Routledge is an imprint of the Taylor & Francis Group, an informa business

British Library Cataloguing-in-Publication Data
A catalogue record for this book is available from the British Library

Library of Congress Cataloging-in-Publication Data
A catalog record has been requested for this book

ISBN: 9780367686000 (hbk)
ISBN: 9780367686024 (pbk)
ISBN: 9781003138259 (ebk)

DOI: 10.4324/9781003138259

Typeset in Times New Roman
by codeMantra

Contents

Foreword

Between six and seven years after the first Scottish Independence Referendum in September 2014, pro-independence elements in Scotland seem to think they are moving toward a second, in the forthcoming year or two. By January 2021, 18 successive opinion polls had returned majorities for independence. Support for the SNP, the larger pro-independence party, in the same polls, was consistently above 50% suggesting an overall majority in the devolved parliament and, in their view, a mandate to call the second referendum. In the event, pro-independence parties won a majority of 15 (72–57) in the May 2021 elections to the Scottish Parliament and plans for a second referendum are underway. The UK government and the Labour Party have, of course, expressed firm opposition to the notion.

The surge in support for both independence and the SNP, in these polls and in the election, has been linked with the pandemic management performance of the SNP administration and, in particular, the leadership of the First Minister, Nicola Sturgeon. The apparent hostility of a majority of Scots toward the UK Prime Minister, Boris Johnson, reported in the same polls, and to the process of leaving the EU, based on the 2016 EU referendum poll where more than 60% of the electorate voted to remain in the EU, were also commonly used in explanation. In addition, there were signs, again in the polls, that groups largely opposed to independence in 2014 – women, migrants, English Scots and Labour supporters – were beginning to move toward support for both the SNP and also the pro-independence Greens.

In sharp contrast to these signs of movement across Scottish society toward support for independence, Scotland's newspapers are largely unmoved. Reader numbers continue to fall but many of the same leading writers remain prominent.

Though diminished, the Scottish press will still be a major influence in the next referendum, on its readers and on the broadcast media reporters who pick-up many of their stories there. Dr David Patrick's *Front-Page Scotland: Newspapers and the Scottish Independence Referendum* will be one of very few substantive sources available to help us understand the part the Scottish press, historically one of the major influencers on political events in Scotland, played in 2014 and might play again in 2021 and beyond.

Though this work is entirely the product of Dr Patrick, he and I have regularly discussed media analysis and its application to the Scottish constitutional debate, in depth and at length, over these seven years. To my knowledge, no one is better placed to speak with authority on the role which the Scottish press played in 2014 and to offer insight into the impact it may have if and when the next referendum on Scottish independence takes place.

Dr John Robertson, Professor of Media Politics and Faculty of Media, Culture and Society, Research Ethics Chair at the University of the West of Scotland until retirement in 2016.

1 Scotland and the press in 2014

In many respects, 2014 seems awfully long ago. Though commentators at the time stressed the uncertainty facing both the domestic and international stages, with the benefit of hindsight the mid-2010s was a period of relative stability. The all-consuming media circus surrounding the Trump presidency had yet to emerge, while the divisive issue of the Brexit campaign and the often-incompetent negotiations which followed had yet to dominate the British news cycle. Of course, the greatest difference in comparison were the relative freedoms and opportunities offered by 2014, still half a decade away from the emergence of the generation-defining issue of coronavirus.

On both a Scottish and UK level there have been a variety of changes, though other aspects have proven remarkably resilient in the period to 2021. The Conservatives remain the party of Government, having won the 2015, 2017 and 2019 general elections, while having went through a series of prime ministers. Conservative leader at the time of the independence referendum, David Cameron's 2016 resignation saw Theresa May assume the role, only for her to be replaced by Boris Johnson in 2019. The years after the independence referendum were dominated by another vote, this being the 2016 referendum on the issue of membership of the European Union, and this has arguably become the defining narrative in British politics in the intervening years (up to the current pandemic, certainly).

At a Scottish level, while the 2014 referendum saw 55% of voters reject independence, the SNP have enjoyed consistent electoral success. The 2015 general election proved something of a high point in this regard, with a post-referendum rise in membership and popularity seeing the party claim 56 of Scotland's 59 Westminster seats. Though never as dominant in subsequent ballots, the SNP has nonetheless established itself as an electoral force in Scotland, again gaining a majority of Scottish seats at the 2017 and 2019 general elections. Beyond party

DOI: 10.4324/9781003138259-1

politics, the abstract concept of independence has remained popular, with opinion polls in recent years showing a tentative shift to a pro-independence majority. At the time of writing, it is likely that the independence question will thus remain a defining issue within Scottish politics for the foreseeable future. Many of the political personalities involved may have changed roles in the time since 2014 (Nicola Sturgeon having been First Minister since late 2014; Alex Salmond taking a backbench role and then returning to found the Alba party in 2021; Gordon Brown and Alistair Darling both retiring from politics; and the leaderships of both the Conservatives and Labour going through multiple iterations, both sides of the border), but several of the key foundational debates, as presented through the media, remain broadly the same.

With these latter points in mind, this monograph will present and analyse newspaper coverage of the 2014 Scottish independence referendum: both as a means of better understanding the key narratives and framing devices which informed the discourse surrounding this important vote, and to allow for tentative predictions to be made about the content and presentation of future discourse regarding Scotland's place within the United Kingdom. As a source for engaging with media representation of the independence debate, the decision to use newspapers for this purpose may strike one as somewhat odd. In a media environment which includes 24-hour rolling TV news, myriad online outlets and social media content providing news and reporting almost in real-time, getting one's news from a printed source (which at best is usually at least one day behind the coverage of comparative media) can seem almost archaic. However, newspapers retain an important place in Scotland's media environment, part of a complex and rapidly evolving ecosystem of content. Many citizens still gain much of their political knowledge from newspapers, and even if those individuals are not regular purchasers of a newspaper they may still be exposed to or influenced by them in the course of an average day (whether that be through reading one 'second-hand', like in a library or on a train, or simply through passively consuming headlines by passing any of the various outlets which stock newspapers).

Discussions of Scotland's media and its role in presenting (and perhaps influencing) the 2014 independence referendum have emerged in the time since the vote, with research from a number of contributors providing the foundations for the work to follow.[1] *Front-Page Scotland* is primarily a discourse analysis, with the main aim of the book being an attempt to present and deconstruct the manner in which major newspaper titles engaged with what was arguably the most important vote in Scotland's history to that point. Though a substantial part of the text concerns the discourse surrounding policy issues, the main theme presented is the focus dedicated to individuals, and how reference to them came to dominate several aspects of the press coverage from the time.

Informing this research is a close reading (and often multiple re-readings) of almost 7,000 individual examples of newspaper content. These included all front pages, news reports, comment and opinion pieces, editorials and letters, providing a wealth of material from which to form an analysis. The date range for this study encompasses the final seven weeks leading to the 18 September vote, and the two weeks following. Specifically, all Monday–Friday editions between 1 August and 1 October 2014 were accessed; with one exception to this being the inclusion of Saturday 20 September, this generally being the first edition of most titles to cover both the definitive result of the vote and the resignation of Alex Salmond. Eight daily newspapers were selected to provide the foundations for this study, having a combined circulation in 2013/14 of c. 710,000 and representing the views of outlets from the tabloid, middle-market and broadsheet formats.[2] In terms of Scottish-only titles (meaning those without a 'main' UK edition), included are the *Herald*, *Scotsman* and *Daily Record*, though in each other instance it should be stressed that it is the Scottish version of each newspaper which is utilised, these being: the *Scottish Daily Mail*, *Scottish Daily Express*, *Times*, *Daily Telegraph* and the *Scottish Sun*. For purposes of brevity, citations of these sources in both the text and references will use a shortened version throughout (e.g. *Telegraph*, *Sun* or *Express*).

This work does not seek to express or disseminate any political position, allegiance or agenda. Instead, it seeks to merely highlight the dominant narrative devices found in the discourse; essentially looking to draw attention to what aspects of the referendum prompted the most press coverage, in addition to providing comment and analysis as to why such trends and observations may have emerged. Further, the work provides speculative discussion regarding the degree to which such trends may inform or shape future debates around independence in the press. Much has indeed changed in the turbulent years since 2014, but press coverage from this period can nonetheless help inform our understanding of media dynamics today.

Notes

1 For example, see: Neil Blain & David Hutchison (eds), *Scotland's Referendum and the Media: National and International Perspectives* (Edinburgh: Edinburgh University Press, 2016); Marina Dekavalla, *Framing*

Referendum Campaigns in the News (Manchester: Manchester University Press, 2018); Marina Dekavalla, "Framing referendum campaigns: The 2014 Scottish independence referendum in the press", *Media, Culture & Society*, Vol. 38 (6), pp. 793–810. Also informative for the purposes of such research are those sources published by journalists: David Torrance, *100 Days of Hope and Fear: How Scotland's Referendum Was Lost and Won* (Edinburgh: Luath Press, 2014); Iain MacWhirter, *Disunited Kingdom: How Westminster Won a Referendum but Lost Scotland* (Glasgow: Cargo Publishing, 2014); Peter Geoghegan, *The People's Referendum: Why Scotland Will Never Be the Same Again* (Edinburgh: Luath Press, 2015).

2 Neil Blain & David Hutchison, "The Media Landscape in Scotland", in Blain & Hutchison, *Scotland's Referendum and the Media*, p. 20.

2   It's the economy, stupit

Presenting an uncertain future

Much of the press focus concerning Scottish independence centred around economics, with several aspects given persistent coverage. Indeed, it was rare to find an edition of any newspaper which did not feature this theme being highlighted in some fashion. This correlates with Marina Dekavalla's statistical findings revealing that the economy frame was among the most dominant within the coverage, with the attention devoted to economics far outweighing press interest afforded themes like self-determination or national division.[1] Journalists would be only one group among many who would focus their attention on these themes, with professional economists, bankers, industrialists and members of the public all contributing some form of commentary: 'Never has there been such a slew of analysis on our economy and our public finances: the laptops of economists have a feverish glow and their keyboards buckle in the heat'.[2] How enlightening these various analyses were, however, is a matter of debate, with virtually all claims from both sides being, at best, informed speculation. This lack of hard facts would inevitably lead to many exaggerated and often baseless assertions, several of which lapsed into hyperbole. Certainly, as Torrance notes, 'The first casualty of the referendum was, inevitably, nuance'.[3]

Heading towards catastrophe?

A dominant theme within press discussion of an independent Scotland's economy was that of uncertainty. Lack of concrete answers from the Yes campaign were seized upon, especially by the more right-wing titles, and regularly highlighted as evidence that independence presented a leap into the economic unknown. Much of this would be justified, given the general inability of humans to accurately predict the future, though others would reference bizarre and unrelated concepts. 'Perhaps English politicians should remind Scottish voters

DOI: 10.4324/9781003138259-2

of the Darien Disaster of the 1690s', argued one submission, 'when the Kingdom of Scotland, in an attempt to break free of what it perceived as English hegemony, bankrupted itself in an attempt to become a world trading nation'.[4] This uncertainty was, in turn, utilised to strengthen the argument that Scotland was destined for economic ruin, with most titles entertaining this notion at some point, if not always actively propagating it. Pro-independence arguments were routinely challenged in such a fashion, with several contributors forthright in their position that Scotland was headed towards economic catastrophe. As Kerry Gill would argue:

> Some will be tempted by the First Minister's empty promises, but most will probably have come to realise that he is a man with a plot rather than a plan, a dream rather than an economic proposal that stands up to the light of day.[5]

Such themes were repeated ad nauseam, with Scotland's supposed impending calamity often explicitly linked to the pronouncements of Alex Salmond. 'Today is D-Day – our chance to ensure our future and that of our families is secure', asserted a *Mail* opinion piece, 'Salmond is like the pied piper. The music is enchanting, but the destination one of disaster'.[6]

Other content was more measured in expressing such concerns, but nonetheless contributed to a generalised notion that Scotland would face serious economic challenges upon becoming an independent state. For example, Greg Philo highlighted that negotiations following a Yes vote would become 'very intense', opining further, 'as the family split becomes bitter, they [rUK] have the capacity to simply pull the plug on our economy'.[7] A letter to the *Herald*, while noting the author 'did not think that anybody [...] can accurately forecast how the economy will look in 10 years', would conclude, 'What is certain is that without a strong economy any promises from Holyrood or Westminster on jobs, social care, child welfare and the NHS will not be met'.[8]

This is not to say that this form of reporting was not criticised. Yes-leaning commentators, especially, were often quick to challenge forecasts of impending economic doom, though such voices tended to be restricted to the pages of the *Herald, Sun, Record* or *Scotsman*. 'Now that the love bombing is over', commented Iain MacWhirter as the campaign entered its final weeks, 'bombs of a different kind will start falling on Scotland in the effort to persuade voters that the UK's offer is one they really cannot afford to refuse'.[9] Though conceivable that such persistent focus on the potential negative consequences of independence may have influenced the decisions of some voters, this cannot be said with any certainty. That these arguments would have an impact on the result did, however, draw limited comment from the press, as in the following *Times* editorial: 'The pledge of extra powers has probably done something to stall nationalism. So has the relentless emphasis on the deleterious economic consequences that will follow from separation'.[10]

Closed for business

In discussing the economic impact of independence, the statements of a variety of businesses were regularly cited. Major firms, including prominent names from energy and banking, saw their concerns gain significant press coverage, often being granted front page exposure. That Scotland faced an undefined future became a key aspect of this reporting, with the concerns of business leaders often (uncritically) highlighted as reason to reject independence:

> Any uncertainty is bad for business, and it is beyond the bounds of credibility to suggest senior figures like David Nish, Standard Life's chief executive, and Sir Ian Wood, the leading expert on North Sea oil, are playing fast and loose, or even playing politics, with such economic dynamite [...] they should not be lightly dismissed.[11]

These fears would inevitably also find expression in the letters pages, with a contribution to the *Mail* lamenting, 'British businesses are facing a period of acute political uncertainty [...] The country we live in, and that firms do business from, could in a few years be a very different place'.[12]

A peak of such reporting came on 11 September, a mere week before the vote, where various businesses came out publicly against the economic prospects of independence. Described by the *Herald* as a 'concerted attack from the UK's political leaders and big business', a number of corporate entities publicly declared that independence carried myriad risks.[13] The *Mail* reported how BP and Shell were 'throwing their weight behind a new warning from oil tycoon Sir Ian Wood that oil reserves in Scotland have been hugely overestimated by the Yes campaign', with a *Record* editorial arguing that 'the real drama of the day came in a series of seismic interventions on the economic front'.[14] Though the press releases from such businesses were discussing the prospects of independence in general, much of the coverage would frame the story as a personal defeat for Alex Salmond, such as in a front page article from Tom Peterkin: 'Alex Salmond was dealt a series of blows yesterday as retailers warned independence could lead to price rises and several Scottish banks unveiled contingency plans that would see them registered in England in the event of a Yes vote'.[15] Such was the personal focus on Salmond in this regard that 10 September was dubbed the First Minister's 'Black Wednesday'. This expression would find its way into various news and comment pieces, appearing prominently on the front pages of the *Record* and the *Express*. Highlighting the level of coordination and collaboration between the No campaign and certain newspapers, this term was actually coined by Better Together, as detailed by Joe Pike:

> At Better Together's headquarters, Danny Alexander and Labour strategy chief Paul Sinclair hatched a plan: this was to be "Alex Salmond's Black Wednesday." Sinclair rang round a long list of journalists to brief them on the snappy sound bite, while Alexander insistently told the team of press officers: "We have to brand this."[16]

Despite the number of businesses evidently voicing their opinions, a further aspect of the coverage claimed that companies were being somehow silenced by the Scottish government, as detailed in the following front page *Telegraph* article: 'More than a hundred Scottish business leaders wanted to sign a letter backing the Union but stayed silent because they feared "consequences" from the SNP Government'.[17]

There were, of course, counterarguments against the claims made by the business community, many surfacing in the letters sections. 'As the independence referendum date draws nearer, the clandestine Tories of the business world are crawling out of the woodwork, warning the nation of the long-term catastrophic impact a Yes victory would have on the economy', lamented a submission to the *Mail*, going on to warn: 'Don't let the orchestrated fear campaign destroy our chance to be an independent nation which will flourish again'.[18] Others would highlight the vested interests of these titans of business, regarding them as an extension of the No campaign: 'Elements of big business have joined the chorus of the scaremongers', remarked a letter to the *Herald*,

> As a No vote pretty much guarantees a continuation of a low-pay economy and a vote for Yes is a vote for a fight on a more even playing field for a high-wage economy, surely only the politically naïve are really surprised by this turn of events.[19]

Cost of living

Though press engagement often described Scotland's potential economic ruin in generalised, macro terms, much of the coverage was also at pains to emphasise the negative impact that would be felt by individual people and their families. The focus on personal finances and the implied risks from independence was a deliberate and open tactic of the No campaign, as reported by Simon Johnson: '[Better Together] will continue to focus on the risks of separation and the Union's economic benefits, along with attempting to persuade Scots that a No vote is just as patriotic as backing separation'.[20] To this end, one aspect of the transition which was highlighted was the start-up costs which Scotland might face. Early September saw several outlets stating that such expenditures had so far been underestimated by the Yes campaign, with the *Mail* citing analysis which argued that 'start-up costs of a separate Scotland would be ten times the amount Alex Salmond has claimed'.[21] Quoting a figure of £2.4 billion, this was equated to a cost of 'about £1,000 for every Scottish household', with some even giving the impression that families would be actively billed for such an amount.[22]

Other potential costs to residents of Scotland were regularly discussed. The provision of pensions, for example, would receive attention, particularly in those outlets which were more right-leaning and had older readerships, such as the *Express*. For example, as a guest column from Labour MP, Gregg McClymont, would argue after the second TV showdown between Salmond and Darling:

> Not a single person watching Monday's TV debate will feel more confident about the security of his or her pension in the event of a yes vote. After all, there is nothing more important in pensions than certainty about in which currency it will be paid.[23]

The impact on house prices and mortgage costs also garnered frequent attention, with the potential for a market crash being a key focal point of such coverage. The *Mail* would report, for example, on a Zoopla analysis which claimed independence 'would slash £85 billion' from the Scottish housing market: 'A Yes vote could wipe £31,000 off the average house price in Scotland in a devastating property crash. The housing industry yesterday warned the country would suffer a second credit crunch in the event of independence'.[24] Concerns over repayments were similarly highlighted, with the *Times* citing experts who 'warned that house prices in Scotland would crash if the country voted for independence as lenders pulled out of the mortgage market', while the *Scotsman* gave front-page credibility to Johann Lamont's claim that independence would cost the 'average family' an 'extra £1,600 a year in mortgage repayments'.[25]

Citing specific figures, while framing them so as to emphasise the personal financial cost to the reader, was undoubtedly used by sections of the press as a means of dissuading a Yes vote. Given that 2014 was only a few years detached from the 2008 financial crisis, this focus on the figures may indeed have been a deliberate and effective means of stressing the costs of independence. A more personal, emotional angle was also utilised, though, with potential costs often described in terms of their impact, specifically, on one's family. This was particularly prevalent in those newspapers which were among the most anti-independence, with such reporting receiving a fair degree of front page exposure. The *Express*, citing the concerns of the chairman of John Lewis, would report how 'Families will face higher shopping bills if Scots voters back independence', with the *Mail* echoing such concerns: 'Major stores yesterday warned Scots families that they will face higher prices on essentials from bread and milk to children's clothes after a Yes vote'.[26] Opinion pieces would continue this trend of framing the concerns of business in relation to the impact on families, such as in the following extract from Kerry Gill:

> Most of us do not gamble. We are careful with our money, as we are with our families' future [...] Mr Salmond is a gambler, at the bookies and by nature and, oh so crucially – and terrifyingly – with Scotland's future.[27]

Such fears would also be repeated in those outlets which were not as diametrically opposed to independence, with a *Sun* editorial arguing, 'the emotional tug of freedom will always be tempered by financial reality. People will, understandably, put themselves and their families first'.[28]

In general terms, coverage discussing the economic prospects of an independent Scotland tended to frame the future as one of uncertainty at best and utter calamity at worst. This would be most pronounced in the *Express*, *Mail* and *Telegraph*, though would form a sizable part of the coverage from most titles. Counterarguments and potential positive consequences of independence did gain some marginal attention in the press, but this tended to be restricted to the comment or letters sections. When economic stories were given front page coverage, these were almost invariably negative about the prospects of independence, and this in itself may have given a passive impression that Scotland's prospects under independence were unconvincing. Large-print headlines can be consumed and assimilated even by those who never purchase nor read a newspaper, simply through individuals being temporarily exposed to such content in the routines of everyday life (especially those who live in a metropolitan area or use public transport). Therefore, it is reasonable to argue that a constant stream of negative stories appearing on page one could well have contributed to a general conceptualisation which saw Scotland's economic prospects as being potentially disastrous; a phenomenon which could have influenced an audience far beyond simply those who actually bought a newspaper.

Slippery topic: debates over oil

North Sea oil was first discovered in the 1970s, and has since been critical to both the UK economy and the case for Scottish independence. Indeed, 'It's Scotland's Oil' became the main slogan of the 1979 referendum on Scottish devolution, and it was unavoidable that the issue would form a key aspect of press debate concerning independence.

A large degree of coverage regarding oil was related to the unpredictability of future extraction, which in turn would of course affect projected revenues. Several news and comment articles speculated over possible remaining reserves, with claims from both campaigns receiving attention to varying degrees. Perhaps the most important intervention in this regard – or at least that which generated the greatest press coverage – was that by Sir Ian Wood.[29] Long-recognised as a leading industry expert, Wood argued that Scottish government projections regarding oil output had been hugely exaggerated, a position which sections of the press were content to accept and disseminate without criticism. Much emphasis was placed on Sir Ian's experience in the industry, positioning his as a voice to be listened to: 'His intervention on Wednesday was hugely significant because oil is a significant plank of the first minister's separation case and Sir Ian is a global expert on the industry'.[30] Such themes were echoed by Peter Jones in the *Herald*, who reported that the 'unpredictability of final value on top of rising costs is why the business mind of Sir Ian Wood, after a lifetime in the industry, thinks we will be doing well to get another 16.5 billion [sic] barrels out'.[31] Others would be even more forthright in their endorsement of Wood's opinions, with a letter to the *Mail* seeing his intervention as all but destroying the economic case for independence. 'Alex Salmond's biggest lie, that an independent Scotland could float onward and upward on the strength of its oil and gas resources, has finally been nailed', asserted Alex Brummer, 'The greatest author-ity on Scottish oil, Sir Ian Wood – together with the bosses of BP and Shell – has exposed it as pure fantasy'.[32] Indeed, Sir Ian would himself pen an article for the *Mail*, published on the day preceding the referen-dum. 'This is probably the most important referendum Scotland will ever have and we must not let our fervour for nationalism overcome our responsibility for providing the best possible economic future and opportunities for our children and grandchildren', warned Sir Ian, 'There will be no new oil bonanza'.[33] This is not to say that all con-tributors were as convinced by projections (from both sides) regarding oil, with occasional comment highlighting the fact that estimates were often unreliable:

> So how much ruddy oil is out there under Scottish waters? [...] the important question is this: how much more oil can be extracted at a profit? And to that question, anybody who tells you that they know the answer is a liar.[34]

Such a position was repeated by Chris Musson of the *Sun*, who opined, 'the truth is no one really knows if we're in for a black gold bonanza – or desperately squeezing the last from the North Sea'.[35]

Related aspects of the oil debate, separate from Wood's comments, were also discussed; one of which was practical considerations of how the industry in an independent Scotland would impact the rest of the United Kingdom. 'Their [rUK] tax revenues will obviously go down if we take it all, and there will be less money to spend on much needed welfare services in places like Newcastle, Manchester, the Welsh Val-leys, and Northern Ireland', wrote one concerned contributor to the *Herald*, elaborating that such a course would 'simply show the world that Scots are greedy, small-minded and uncaring'.[36] Commentary would also make the argument that ownership of Scottish oil would have to be counterbalanced with competing claims on the British pound. Addressing this, Colin Cookson wrote in the *Mail*:

> So the end game must be, if it is Scotland's pound, it's the UK's oil. It cannot be the case that, if a split comes, one side gets the assets in the bank while the other has shared use of the bank book.[37]

This theme was prominent at various times in the same publication, with another comment article criticising that Alex Salmond 'has threatened to take on no debt but thinks he will get 100 per cent of the oil. The real world is not like that'.[38] Such claims were, as expected, popular among those who had decided to vote No and often cited as evidence that the plans of the Yes campaign had been fundamentally undermined: 'The SNP's original vision of building a wealthy Scandinavian-style society on such a basis is now dead on the Continental Shelf'.[39]

Certainly, there were occasional arguments regarding oil from those supporting a Yes vote, but these were far less frequent than the counter-positions cited. Joan McAlpine would be one such voice who, responding to the question 'Will we be too dependent on oil if we choose independence?', asserted: 'Even without oil, Scotland's wealth is around the same as the rest of the UK, according to official figures [...] But the oil is a huge bonus and gives Scotland a great head start'.[40] This was repeated in a letter to the *Herald*, which argued,

> In the past few decades more than 100 countries around the world have taken the decision to become independent, almost none of them with the wealth of natural resources, the economic opportunities and the established social infrastructure that we already have in Scotland.[41]

Rather than citing the positive case for oil, others would instead challenge the neutrality of those claiming that the resource was rapidly dwindling. 'When I see Sir in front of someone's name, I think back to a bunch of Lords who sold Scotland out at the Union of the Crowns', remarked one letter, 'Contrary to what Sir Ian Wood says, as far as I can ascertain, he is, in fact, backing the No campaign. Such a parcel of rogues in a nation'.[42]

Though the debates concerning the potential of oil in an independent Scotland dominated coverage of Scotland's energy resources, a handful of articles focused on other sectors. Among these was the emerging field of fracking, which by 2014 had become well-established in the US and brought about remarkable returns in those states it had found a foothold. The *Sun* described the possibilities presented by this new industry in glowing terms, being one of the only outlets to do so: 'A North Sea fracking revolution could net up to £600 billion for an independent Scotland in a "new black gold bonanza", a new report claims'.[43] Other newspapers presented the story with a greater degree of caution, with the *Times* highlighting in a front page article that the conclusion of said report had been 'attacked as pure guesswork by a leading energy academic and described as "a huge if" by the one independent oil company that is hoping to explore the resource's potential'.[44] The long-term viability of prioritising oil resources was also questioned, drawing attention to the lack of focus devoted to alternative energy possibilities. One such letter argued that Scotland 'desperately needs to divert human brains from the search for oil to the search for alternatives; and that means building Scotland's future on something other than her stock of highly pollutant fuels'.[45] Another, far more critical of the energy policy of an independent Scotland, complained how they had 'heard nothing regarding renewable energy and how the subsidies will be afforded', going on to stress, 'If our energy bills or our taxes must increase to pay the subsidies [...] then the result will be greater fuel poverty'.[46]

Though a minority opinion, Peter Jones would go further than most, actively arguing against the continued exploitation of oil:

> It is becoming increasingly clear that if there is to be a boost, or more realistically a maintenance, of living standards, Scotland will need to produce every last ounce of oil and gas. Yet if we do that, we will also be helping planet-wrecking climate change.

Jones would further opine, 'Personally in view of the dire consequences of what would be inflicted on my children and grandchildren, I think I would become a militant greenie to stop North Sea shale oil happening'.[47] The focus on energy sources other than oil, however, was rarely given an airing during the debate, a notable observation given Scotland's established possibilities in terms of renewables, such as wind or tidal power. Indeed, discussions of renewable energy options were relevant only by their absence, with oil evidently framed as the only game in town. Such debates, over the amount of remaining oil and the volatility of its price, continued long after the referendum, and will no doubt become a key focal point of coverage once again should a second referendum take place.

Notes

1 Marina Dekavalla, "Framing referendum campaigns: The 2014 Scottish independence referendum in the press", *Media, Culture & Society*, Vol. 38 (6), p. 805.
2 Bill Jamieson, "Yes or No, questions will continue", *Scotsman*, 14.8.14, p. 25.
3 David Torrance, *100 Days of Hope and Fear: How Scotland's Referendum Was Won and Lost* (Edinburgh: Luath Press, 2014), p. 19.
4 Peter Forrest, "Is the currency the only issue of substance?", *Times*, 12.9.14, p. 27.
5 Kerry Gill, "Desperate Salmond will say anything to con Scottish voters", *Express*, 14.8.14, p. 12.

6 Ewen Stewart, "Go it alone and we can expect most volatile economy in Europe", *Mail*, 18.9.14, p. 11.
7 Greg Philo, "Salmond won the plaudits, but he did not win the debate", *Herald*, 27.8.14, p. 14.
8 Mel Green, "Time for us to take responsibility and stop blaming Westminster", *Herald*, 17.9.14, p. 18.
9 Iain MacWhirter, "This 'effing referendum' is far from over yet, I swear", *Herald*, 11.9.14, p. 13.
10 Editorial, "Money talks", *Times*, 12.9.14, p. 26.
11 Catherine MacLeod, "There is only one real Team Scotland", *Herald*, 11.9.14, p. 15.
12 Ruth Sutherland, "Businesses must speak out", *Mail*, 29.8.14, p. 73.
13 Magnus Gardham & Helen Puttick, "Union turns the heat on Yes", *Herald*, 11.9.14, p. 1.
14 Victoria Allen, "Blow to SNP as BP and Shell throw weight behind the UK", 11.9.14, p. 9; Editorial, "Salmond cornered by economic fears", *Daily Record*, 11.9.14, p. 10.
15 Tom Peterkin, "Company chiefs in Yes vote warnings", *Scotsman*, 12.9.14, p. 1.
16 Joe Pike, *Project Fear: How An Unlikely Alliance Left a Kingdom United but a Country Divided* (London: Biteback Publishing, 2015), p. 131; Torcuil Crichton, "Alex's Black Wednesday", *Record*, 11.9.14, p. 1.
17 Ben Riley-Smith, "Business leaders 'fear SNP backlash'", *Telegraph*, 28.8.14, p. 1.
18 Lorna Bryan, "Show me the money", *Mail*, 27.8.14, p. 62.
19 Bill Ramsay, "We risk being cast as outcasts if we retain all the oil revenues", *Herald*, 12.9.14, p. 18.
20 Simon Johnson, "Gordon Brown joins campaign trail", *Telegraph*, 8.9.14, p. 6.
21 Gareth Rose, "£1,000 bill for every family", *Mail*, 1.9.14, p. 1.
22 Hamish Macdonell, "True cost of setting up new nation would be £2.4bn, says think-tank", *Times*, 1.9.14, p. 6.
23 Gregg McClymont, "Scots pensioners can't depend on SNP's promises", *Express*, 27.8.14, p. 12.
24 Victoria Allen, "Yes vote may spark house price freefall", *Mail*, 16.9.14, p. 9.
25 Philip Aldrick & Hamish Macdonell, "Scots householders at risk of price crash as the markets panic", *Times*, 9.9.14, p. 6; Andrew Whitaker, "'Mortgage up £1,600 if Scotland votes Yes'", *Scotsman*, 11.8.14, p. 1.
26 Dean Herbert, "Vote 'Yes' for higher prices", *Express*, 12.9.14, p. 1; Alan Simpson, "Families face cost of living crisis if UK splits", *Mail*, 12.9.14, p. 1.
27 Kerry Gill, "Comment", *Express*, 6.8.14, p. 4.
28 Editorial, "Give us some answers, Alex", *Sun*, 7.8.14, p. 6.
29 Riley-Smith, "Salmond refuses to back down", *Telegraph*, 22.8.14, p. 13.
30 Lindsay McIntosh, "Salmond called to account for oil forecasts", *Times*, 22.8.14, p. 13.
31 Peter Jones, "The truth about oil? Nobody knows", *Scotsman*, 26.8.14, p. 23.
32 Alex Brummer, "Nailing Salmond's lies on oil wealth", *Mail*, 11.9.14, p. 69.
33 Sir Ian Wood, "As you cast your vote be sure of one thing: There will be no oil bonanza", *Mail*, 17.9.14, p. 9.
34 Jones, "The truth about oil?"
35 Chris Musson, "Black gold's crucial role", *Sun*, 4.9.14, p. 8.

36 MG Williamson, "We risk being cast as outcasts if we retain all the oil revenues", *Herald*, 12.9.14, p. 18.

37 Colin Cookson, "If you share the pound, you must share oil too", *Express*, 25.8.14, p. 42.

38 Stewart, "Go it alone".

39 Brummer, "Nailing Salmond's lies".

40 Joan McAlpine, "Exposing London's lies about Scots oil wealth", *Record*, 20.8.14, p. 13.

41 Iain AD Mann, "Time for us to take responsibility and stop blaming Westminster", *Herald*, 17.9.14, p. 18.

42 T Gardner, "You would expect Sir Ian to back the No campaign", *Express*, 25.8.14, p. 42.

43 Chris Musson, "£600bn? That's a fracking fortune", *Sun*, 4.9.14, p. 8.

44 Lindsay McIntosh & Peter Jones, "North Sea 'will earn £300bn for Scotland'", *Times*, 5.9.14, p. 1.

45 Donald Macleod, "Lots of rhetoric from Salmond, but few hard facts", *Express*, 8.9.14, p. 12.

46 Lyndsey Ward, "Scotland's energy bill", *Telegraph*, 3.9.14, p. 21.

47 Peter Jones, "Essential oil burns a hole in idealism", *Scotsman*, 9.9.14, p. 21.

3   What matters most

The health service and currency

Debating the NHS

Being one of the largest employers in Scotland, coupled with its position as a social institution, it was unsurprising that the NHS became a crucial topic within the independence debate. This focus was especially notable in that the NHS was one of the few areas of contention in which current performance, as opposed to speculation about the future, was discussed. Particularly in the *Express* – which has an older readership, who would be expected to be more frequent users of the health service – critique of the contemporary management of Scotland's health service gained infrequent though prominent coverage. An editorial asserted that it was 'clear that the Scottish Government – having poured every last ounce of energy into the referendum debate, its ministers dispatched far and wide to preach the evils of the United Kingdom – is neglecting its basic duty', further concluding, 'the NHS works despite SNP ministers rather than because of them'.[1] Such themes would be repeated in letters from readers, with one example arguing: 'If anybody is still in any doubt about the security of the NHS in Scotland after a Yes vote I would bet they have not experienced the decline in the service at the present time'.[2] A notable angle came from the *Telegraph*, in a series of front page articles from early September revealing that NHS Scotland contracts had been awarded to a private slimming company. Given the Yes campaign's warnings about the creeping privatisation of the health service, these details were cited as evidence of SNP hypocrisy: '[Alex Salmond's] political opponents said he was scaring the vulnerable with lurid warnings, while at the same time "nodding through NHS contracts to independent providers"'.[3] Despite the exclusive story appearing prominently in the *Telegraph*, however, it failed to gain significant traction in other outlets, including those which were actively promoting a No vote.

DOI: 10.4324/9781003138259-3

More generally, the NHS continued to be debated in relation to what would happen to the institution following a Yes vote. Many notable figures on the No side deliberately invoked the NHS in their campaigning, with David Cameron arguing that UK increases in health spending had not been replicated in Scotland due to SNP policies, while Nick Clegg concerned himself with the affordability of the NHS should Scotland become independent: 'There would be less money to spend on essential services like the NHS. I don't want that for Scotland'.[4] Gordon Brown would be the most vocal politician in this regard, however, regularly invoking his own personal experiences to defend his pro-Union position:

> The First Minister has made the NHS a major campaign issue, warning that it would be under threat of "privatisation and fragmentation" if Scotland stayed within the United Kingdom. But, close to tears as he said the NHS saved his sight following a childhood rugby accident and looked after a dying Jennifer, Mr Brown dismissed this.[5]

Indeed, Brown's comments on the NHS would gain regular front page exposure, such as in an article which began, 'Gordon Brown yesterday invoked the memory of his dead infant daughter to "nail the SNP lie" over the future of the health service in Scotland'.[6] With Brown's campaigning in particular, the NHS would thus become a key strategic issue used to win over Labour voters and older members of the electorate. A small number of news articles highlighted an aspect of the story focusing on those supporting a Yes vote, though these were invariably relegated to smaller, inside-page mentions; generally, the bulk of the coverage was critical of pro-independence claims surrounding the future of the NHS.

That the NHS became a main issue in the independence debate was, in part, due to the fact that the Yes campaign (the SNP especially) pushed this particular angle in its quest to win over undecided voters. Gaining increased prominence following the first televised debate between Alex Salmond and Alistair Darling, this development drew comment from various newspapers: 'The SNP is keen to put the future of the health service at the heart of the independence campaign after polling showed the issue could sway undecided voters to back Yes'.[7] The *Record* would also devote editorial space to the issue. 'The stakes are too high, passions are too inflamed and the consequences too important for every possible trick not to be pulled', noted a lead article, 'It has become clear that part of Alex Salmond's strategy over the next four weeks is to warn about the future of health provision if Scotland votes No'.[8] Others commented that such an approach was appearing to win support for independence in the final weeks of the campaign, with Alan Cochrane of the *Telegraph* highlighting how the 'rise in support for the separatists over the late summer has coincided with their decision to focus on health as their main weapon in this bitter, and now increasingly close, contest'.[9]

In terms of opinion on the future of Scotland's NHS, the vast majority sought to dismiss or challenge the positions of Alex Salmond and the wider Yes campaign. Indeed, with the exception of currency, there were few other pro-independence assertions which received such concentrated criticism. As health policy was already devolved by 2014, and as such was solely the responsibility of the Scottish government, several pro-Union contributors were quick to critique claims that the Scottish NHS was in danger of being negatively impacted upon by budget cuts from Westminster. Again, the *Express* ran with this angle more than most, with several editorial columns devoted to challenging the contention that the NHS would be safer in an independent Scotland. One such piece argued that Salmond 'had his bluff thoroughly called over his shameful scaremongering about the future of the NHS', building on a lead article appearing few days earlier: 'Voters in Scotland are about to make a decision that will have a deep and lasting effect on their future, and the future of generations to come. The least they deserve is honesty from the First Minister'.[10] Emphasising that the SNP were supposedly lying in spreading such claims, a related piece would argue that 'Alex Salmond, Nicola Sturgeon and their colleagues know perfectly well that there is no threat whatsoever to the wholly devolved service in Scotland from Westminster', while another editorial stressed that the entire pro-independence campaign was being deliberately loose with the facts:

> Yes Scotland campaigners are adept at spreading untruths about the future of Scotland's health service. Their cynical exploitation of the NHS – nurtured by all the main political parties in equal measure – has become their latest weapon in trying to scare Scots into voting Yes next month.[11]

Such criticism was not restricted to editorial space, with pro-Union commentary also pouring scorn on the idea that the NHS was under threat. Dismissing Yes campaign claims about the NHS as blatant lies, Alex Massie, writing in the *Times*, would assert, 'it is clear that dishonesty has replaced optimism and scaremongering has supplanted decency as the Yes campaign hurtles towards its date with destiny'.[12] Such views were repeated by Jackson Carlaw – who would go on to become leader of the Scottish Conservatives for a short period in 2020 – in a guest piece for the *Express*. 'I can only assume the First Minister hopes some vulnerable voters who depend on the NHS will be intimidated enough to swallow this nonsense', commented Carlaw, 'This surely tells us everything about the contempt in which he holds the people of Scotland. Say anything, however lurid, however false, to scare up a few Yes votes come September'.[13] Perhaps tellingly, there were virtually no substantial editorials or comment pieces which argued against these positions, with pro-independence voices on the matter distinctly rare. Those counterclaims which did appear were generally restricted to the letters pages, such as with the following *Herald* submission:

> I am not frightened by the inevitable uncertainties that face any newly independent nation. But I am terrified by the belief that if we continue as we are it will be my grandson, or his children, who will face life – and death – without the NHS.[14]

Criticism of pro-independence claims surrounding the NHS was utilised to argue a further point, that the focus on health was evidence that the Yes campaign had ran out of ideas. As a *Record* editorial would state, 'down in the polls, without an answer about what currency we will use if we can't have the pound, they will suddenly insist only a Yes vote will protect the health service'.[15] Describing NHS claims as 'the biggest red herring yet in the referendum debate', a lead article in the same newspaper would go on to remark, 'No wonder critics call it a "desperate" tactic from a man [Salmond] who knows he is losing'.[16] That the Yes campaign was growing desperate became a persistent theme in the coverage, with one *Express* editorial, written a few weeks after the first televised debate, asserting:

> Ever since Alistair Darling destroyed Alex Salmond's myth of a fiscal union with the rest of the UK live on television, the First Minister has been seeking a new plank on which to base his increasingly desperate separatist hopes […] He has decided to peddle the erroneous line that a Yes vote is the only way to save the NHS from being privatised.[17]

Describing privatisation of the NHS as 'the big bogeyman of the referendum', Labour MSP Kezia Dugdale, in her regular column for the *Record*, echoed such criticism, 'The Yes campaign's lie about our health service being doomed by a No vote is the last refuge of the desperate. Putting the frighteners on the sick, the elderly and the worried is all they have left'.[18] Writing only a few days before this piece, Jackson Carlaw would demonstrate the similarity between the positions of the Conservatives and Labour on this issue:

> The SNP's shameless behaviour on the NHS in recent weeks has proved the most despicable of many lows in this referendum campaign. Desperate Nationalists will have had this nonsense up their sleeves for months, ready to spin the moment the opinion polls swung against them.[19]

Whether the views of the press on this matter had any particular impact on the way people voted is unclear, but focus on the health service nonetheless featured prominently in the coverage of the referendum. Particularly in those titles which were pro-Union, critiquing pro-independence claims about the NHS became a dominant theme, emerging most frequently in editorial and comment sections. Should the question of independence be once again put to a referendum – especially if this were to take place in the next decade – it is likely that the NHS will once again become an important focal point of the coverage. Indeed, given the increased attention on the health service as a result of its role in combatting the coronavirus pandemic, this could well become a defining issue in any future debate.

On the money: currency

Though themes such as the cost of living, the future of the oil industry and the prospects of the NHS in an independent Scotland were each to receive consistent scrutiny in the weeks leading to the vote, the most prominent economic aspect of the debate was the issue of currency. Chancellor George Osborne, publicly endorsed by the major UK parties, explicitly ruled out a currency union several months before the referendum, but the issue remained contested and unresolved for the duration of the debate. Given that it had the potential to impact upon virtually all other issues, the theme of currency can be justifiably cited as among the most important debates to inform the referendum saga. Certainly, some outlets were quick to link the changing prospects of a currency union to fluctuations in the polls, such as in the following *Times* editorial, appearing less than a week before the vote. 'During the period in which the Yes vote rose quickly, so did optimism about family finances, to the point that as many people thought independence would be good for the domestic budget as thought it would be bad', opined the lead article, 'Now the proportion of Scots who think they would be worse off under independence has risen eight points in a week'.[20] Attention was also drawn to the fact that concerns over currency were already having a negative impact on the markets, often directly explaining this in terms of the impact which this could have on the finances of the average citizen. The *Mail*, for example, commenting upon a dip in the pound, would editorialise:

> At a stroke, every Briton – north and south of the border – knows now that this referendum is no mere academic discussion. It matters to every one of us as it affects the pound in our pocket; it affects our savings; it affects our pensions; it affects our holidays; it affects the companies for which we work.[21]

This is not to say that there were not also (minority) voices frustrated at the fact that the debate had in some ways become myopically focused on this single issue. As a contribution to the *Herald* lamented: 'We are in danger of reducing our nation to the size of a bank note. It seems that the only thing that matters is our currency'.[22]

By far the most persistent feature of the currency debate was criticism of the position taken by the SNP, that Scotland would seek a formal currency union with the United Kingdom. Given particular attention from those outlets openly supporting a No vote, public statements from bankers, economists and other experts were seized upon in order to emphasise the uncertainty which an independent Scotland could face as a result of the currency issue remaining unresolved: 'One of the world's leading economists has warned the poor will suffer the most if voters back independence on Thursday because an independent Scotland will lack creditworthiness on the international markets'.[23] Related reports would also highlight the financial ruin Scotland was expected to face in the event of a currency union, even if agreed upon, failing in the long-term. As Lindsey McIntosh would report,

> Taxpayers in an independent Scotland would be hit with a £30 billion bill if Alex Salmond got his way on a currency union with the rest of the UK, because the deal would "inevitably break up", sending shockwaves through the economy, an expert has warned.[24]

The policies and public pronouncements of Alex Salmond gained particular attention in this regard. His comments would be remarked upon, deconstructed and criticised at length; one of which being his argument that Scotland, without a currency union, would no longer be responsible for its proportion of UK debt:

> Mr Salmond has threatened to walk away from Scotland's share of UK debt if he cannot secure a share of assets, including the currency. Mr Cameron described the ultimatum as "one of the most chilling things that has been said" in the whole referendum debate.[25]

Editorials and comment also regularly criticised the currency plans of the official Yes campaign, with many a lead article utilised to discredit the currency model espoused by the SNP leadership. 'A Yes vote would cause huge upsets in the financial world which, obviously, could filter down to the most modest saver', warned an *Express* article, 'Alex Salmond's abject failure to come clean on the currency a separate Scotland would use [...] is causing widespread uncertainty'.[26] Similar worries were expressed by the *Scotsman*'s editorial:

> The last thing anyone needs is a period of UK financial instability after a Yes vote, with market concerns about the future political and economic governance of the pound. And yet, in the current political climate, this looks to be a very real risk.[27]

Others drew attention to the fact that Scotland, as only one constituent nation of the United Kingdom, would have to be realistic about the prospects of securing a currency union with the blessing of rUK. 'And if we are taking sovereign wills here, why is the Scottish sovereign wish the only one that matters?', queried a comment piece in the *Scotsman*, 'Aren't the people of England, Wales and Northern Ireland allowed a sovereign wish as well?'[28]

Many letters and opinion pieces continued to simply insist that Scotland would under no circumstances be granted a currency union, arguing that to believe the UK government's position merely a bluff was to court potential catastrophe. However, others took a different perspective; tentatively accepting that a currency union was not impossible, while emphasising that the reality of such an agreement would mean Scotland would not, in practical terms, be truly independent. Commenting on the possibility that Scotland could use the pound informally as a transition measure, the *Mail* would opine:

> Keeping our pound without a fiscal agreement with the rest of the UK would leave us no control over interest rates, and devaluation [...] would be beyond us. We would be a laughing stock before the ink was dry on the separation treaty.[29]

Such a position would be echoed in letters to this same title with notable regularity, especially in the days surrounding the two main televised debates. 'So if we don't have our own currency, and don't have our own central bank that can set our interest rates', argued one submission, 'we won't be independent at all in reality'.[30] Several commentators agreed with this analysis, with Peter Jones arguing, 'All the evidence which has piled up on this question points to a simple conclusion – Scotland can have a currency union or independence, but not both'.[31] Further analyses would continue the line of thinking that the currency proposals forwarded by the SNP were indeed workable, but hardly compatible with stated plans for an independent Scotland. 'For what it's worth, I happen to believe that realpolitik would dictate that some sort of currency union would eventually follow a Yes vote', wrote David Torrance for the *Herald*, 'although with terms and conditions that would heavily undermine the central goals of an SNP government'.[32] The concept linking much of this discourse, mirrored in the discussion of other main issues related to the independence debate, was that little could be said about currency with any degree of certainty; a position which, in itself, essentially supported an entrenched narrative (of the future being unknowable and thus dangerously uncertain) being disseminated by the No campaign.

Related to the focus on currency was the prospect of large-scale capital flight from Scotland, a worrying possibility which was given credence by a variety of newspapers. This was partly influenced by the comments of the Governor of The Bank of England, Mark Carney, who revealed in mid-August that the institution had made contingency plans in the event of a Yes majority emerging. Despite the fact that it made sense that such ideas should have been considered, many in the press cited these revelations as evidence of impending financial catastrophe, with several reports on this theme receiving prominent front page exposure: 'Governor Mark Carney yesterday said he had plans to protect the country's financial institutions, as concerns were raised about the possibility of a run on Scottish banks'.[33] Other banking institutions would propagate similar concerns, which were often framed in near-apocalyptic terms, echoing language used to describe the 2008 run on Northern Rock. For example, as the *Telegraph* reported on the words of Douglas Flint: 'The chairman of HSBC today warns that independence risks devastating the Scottish economy by triggering a "flight" of money to England caused by uncertainty over the pound'.[34] These developments were further linked to contemporary concerns about fluctuations in the pound, with an Alan Roden piece in the *Mail* asserting that such 'tremors' were 'the first evidence of the economic consequences of separation'.[35]

Commentators in various forums would further emphasise the supposed impact of the continuing uncertainty, with many arguing that massive capital flight from Scotland was already underway. One such piece came from Bill Jamieson, who somewhat exaggerated the situation in the week before the vote:

> Good morning, Scotland. The whooshing sounds you may hear today are not one of those EU-banned vacuum cleaners. It's the sound of money fast leaving Scotland on fears over next week's referendum outcome. Bank accounts, sterling deposits and pension savings are on the move.[36]

A notable, and at times rather misguided, component of such opinion was the insistence that the economic disaster set to befall Scotland would occur immediately after a Yes vote had been secured. Indeed, some letters went as far as to imply that Scotland would be without a viable currency on 19 September, a lapse into hyperbole which was rarely, if ever, challenged. 'Scotland faces waking up on September 19 without any feasible currency if the "yes" votes wins', wrote one letter to the *Times*, which went on to conclude that the 'argument for an independent Scotland is lost already on the currency issue alone'.[37] Such a position would be echoed in the *Mail*, raising a number of frightful though arguably ill-informed questions regarding Scotland's immediate economic future:

> May I ask all those who may be voting Yes or thinking about it, what are you going to do the day and weeks after the referendum, should Salmond win? I am referring to your money in your pocket, bank, shares, savings and pension. How much will it be worth, if anything?[38]

With the currency question so integral to the debate and receiving such a degree of negative reporting, it was inevitable that there would be rebuttals from those supporting a Yes vote. Though far fewer in number than those arguing against independence, as well as being given less prominent placing in the titles in which they appeared, such contributions nonetheless provided a series of counterpoints to the dominant narrative. A prominent advocate in this respect was Ian Bell, who regularly challenged claims over currency in his *Herald* column.

In one such piece, Bell argued that making the issue of currency the focal point of the No campaign had been shown to have limited impact on voting intentions. 'Currency was supposed to be the killer blow for the No camp. At the first attempt, the Westminster parties, united in obduracy, were supposed scare us into compliance when they ruled out any possibility of a sterling union', commented Bell, 'Then Mr Darling and his allies were supposed to expose Mr Salmond as a man who had not bothered to think things through [...] As things stand, neither tactic has done the trick'.[39] In another article, the same author would highlight that, despite assertions to the contrary, the overall approach of the No campaign was at odds with what it claimed to be the case: 'The mantra of "no pre-negotiation" can be ignored. There has been plenty of that, albeit written in headlines involving the currency, immigration and other things'.[40] Yes-leaning contributors also critiqued the degree to which the position of the UK government regarding a form of currency union would be acted upon in the event of an independence majority. Writing for the *Scotsman*, Hugh Reilly would contribute by relaying his own experiences of having Scottish notes accepted in London: 'The observable truth of how a real economy operates demonstrates the absurdity of Better Together's position that an independent Scotland should be denied the use of sterling'.[41] Readers' letters also challenged the stated position on currency, with some arguing that concerns over the issue were due to fears over the value of the pound in rUK, rather than resulting from worries over the financial implications for an independent Scotland. 'Sometimes when a political choice has to be made it is useful to look at your opponents' views. Often the one they appear to despise and disparage is the one they fear', insisted one such submission, going on to say of the STV showdown between Salmond and Darling, 'In the context of the currency, it was noticeable in Tuesday's debate that Alistair Darling was quick to dismiss the idea of a Scotland using the pound outwith a currency union'.[42]

Indeed, the issue of currency from a pro-independence perspective would gain a more intense hearing in the letters pages than was generally the case in the main sections of the newspapers, with several contributions either making a positive case for Scotland having its own currency or directly challenging the stated position of the UK government and the No campaign. Linking control of the money supply to prospects for the health service, Dr Wilson from NHS for Yes stated in the *Herald*: 'By far the most important aspects predicting the future of NHS Scotland lies in budget considerations. Independence will give Scotland the ability to set her own priorities and the financial resources to carry these through'.[43] Essentially a discussion about money, references to the supposed thrifty nature of the Scots were also invoked, with allusions to being 'canny' cropping up in a handful of submissions. 'By voting Yes', argued the author of a letter to the *Herald*, 'canny Scots have an opportunity to redefine the nature of banking in Scotland, and reduce our exposure to the temptations of international casino banking'.[44] A submission to the *Sun*, slightly more tongue-in-cheek, would present the following related aspect:

> In England, [Darling] is restricted to an English £50 note. However, if he digs deep, he may find a Scottish £100 note, approved by the Bank of England. Why has it got more faith in the Scots having £100 bank notes? Could it be the Scots are more canny with their cash than the spendthrift Westminster Government?[45]

A fundamental part of any economy, that the issue of currency would come to inform and shape much of the independence debate in the press was to be expected. Whether such discussions would take a similar form should a second independence referendum take place is a matter for speculation, but one can safely assume that this critical issue – particularly as the UK economy has come under various pressures resulting from the coronavirus pandemic – will rarely be far from the surface should Scotland's constitutional future be once again placed in the hands of the electorate.

Notes

1 Editorial, "It's Alex Salmond who is neglecting health service", *Express*, 27.8.14, p. 12.
2 Enid Nicholas, "NHS is not safe with nationalists", *Express*, 17.9.14, p. 25.
3 Auslan Cramb, "SNP 'duplicity' as NHS contract goes to US slimming firm", *Telegraph*, 1.9.14, p. 1.
4 Nick Clegg, "More tax, spending and welfare powers for Holyrood parly", *Record*, 16.9.14, p. 5.
5 Paul Gilbride, "Brown: NHS will be safe with us", *Express*, 10.9.14, p. 5.
6 Paul Gilbride, "Brown blasts Salmond's lies on NHS", *Express*, 10.9.14, p. 1.
7 Scott MacNab, "NHS 'starved of resources after No vote", *Scotsman*, 9.9.14, p. 8.
8 Editorial, "Nationalist NHS fears unfounded", *Record*, 20.8.14, p. 6.
9 Alan Cochrane, "The Nats' NHS lie is the biggest in a war full of whoppers. So why is it working?", *Telegraph*, 8.9.14, p. 6.
10 Editorial, "Parliament closes with Salmond the poor loser", *Express*, 22.8.14, p. 12; Editorial, "Salmond's NHS nonsense", *Express*, 18.8.14, p. 12.

11 Editorial, "Why Salmond won't be apologising for NHS lies", *Express*, 17.9.14, p. 12; Editorial, "It's Alex Salmond who is neglecting the health service", *Express*, 27.8.14, p. 12.
12 Alex Massie, "NHS claims are laughable scaremongering", *Times*, 20.8.14, p. 25.
13 Jackson Carlaw, "Scaring vulnerable people with NHS lies is beneath contempt", *Express*, 22.8.14, p. 12.
14 Alice Timmons, "Concerns over the NHS will be addressed after a Yes victory", *Herald*, 22.8.14, p. 14.
15 Editorial, "Operation NHS is Nat convincing", *Record*, 25.8.14, p. 8.
16 Editorial, "Nationalist NHS fears unfounded".
17 Editorial, "Salmond's NHS nonsense".
18 Kezia Dugdale, "Don't fall for the NHS scare stories", *Record*, 25.8.14, p. 8.
19 Carlaw, "Scaring vulnerable people".
20 Editorial, "Money talks".
21 Editorial, "Markets say No", *Mail*, 3.9.14, p. 16.
22 Ada McDonald, "The English are not as engaged in our debate as they should be", *Herald*, 18.8.14, p. 14.
23 David Maddox, "Burden of economic insecurity will fall on poor", *Scotsman*, 15.9.14, p. 9.
24 Lindsay McIntosh, "Scots 'facing £30bn bill' if Salmond gets his way", *Times*, 11.8.14, p. 1.
25 Hamish Macdonell, "Homeowners will suffer if Scotland defaults on debts, voters are warned", *Times*, 4.9.14, p. 15.
26 Editorial, "Proof of financial peril", *Express*, 14.8.14, p. 12.
27 Editorial, "Carney's comments welcome amid uncertainty", *Scotsman*, 14.8.14, p. 26.
28 Peter Jones, "Independence or the pound: which?", *Scotsman*, 12.8.14, p. 25.
29 Editorial, "Currency confusion", *Mail*, 19.8.14, p. 14.
30 Guus Van Goethem, "Show me the money", *Mail*, 27.8.14, p. 62.
31 Jones, "Independence or the pound".
32 David Torrance, "Plan B is not as simple an issue as some might think", *Herald*, 11.8.14, p. 13.
33 Scott MacNab, "Carney ready for a run on Scots banks after Yes", *Scotsman*, 14.8.14, p. 1.
34 Ben Wright & Simon Johnson, "Bank chief: separation a threat to economy", *Telegraph*, 22.8.14, p. 1.
35 Alan Roden, "Pound hit by Yes vote fears", *Mail*, 3.9.14, p. 1.
36 Bill Jamieson, "Countdown to constitutional crisis", *Scotsman*, 11.9.14, p. 29.
37 Elizabeth Oakley, "Is the currency the only issue of substance?", *Times*, 12.9.14, p. 27.
38 James B Borland, "Citizenship scandal", *Mail*, 6.8.14, p. 54.
39 Ian Bell, "Currency question is not frightening off the voters", *Herald*, 20.8.14, p. 13.
40 Ian Bell, "English indifference to our vote is hard to understand", *Herald*, 3.9.14, p. 15.
41 Hugh Reilly, "As the man said, this won't affect the pound in your pocket", *Scotsman*, 26.8.14, p. 24.
42 Donald MacRae, 'First Minister should call Better Together's bluff over the pound", *Herald*, 8.8.14, p. 16.

43 Dr Willie Wilson, "Gordon Brown's intervention will do nothing to safe-guard the future of the health service in Scotland", *Herald*, 11.9.14, p. 16.
44 Joe Darby, "We risk being cast as outcasts if we retain all the oil revenues", *Herald*, 12.9.14, p. 18.
45 Terry Duncan, "Make Anne the Princess of Scotland", *Sun*, 12.8.14, p. 37.

4 Scotland's place in the world

Military and strategic considerations

Economic issues, as illustrated, came to dominate much of the coverage of the referendum, with claim and counterclaim endlessly publicised, propagated or critiqued. Another dominant thematic cluster, however, would be discussion over both Scotland's military prospects and the country's expectations with regard to joining a variety of international institutions. Though there were exceptions, it is observed that much of the press engagement with these issues tended to frame an independent Scotland as being weakened in several respects. Membership of various organisations and alliances was repeatedly put in doubt, combined with a persistent narrative arguing that Scotland would also be more vulnerable to attack from hostile parties.

The question of defence

The matter of how an independent Scotland would defend itself became a semi-regular feature of the coverage from the referendum period, with much of the discourse emphasising the inherent risks to the security of both Scotland and the United Kingdom. These themes would feature on the front pages far less frequently than issues surrounding economics, but nonetheless generated considerable press coverage, gaining particular attention in the letters sections.

An important component of this narrative was the question over Nato membership, with the prospects of an independent Scotland being immediately welcomed back into the alliance being seen as somewhat dubious. For example, the concerns of Sir Richard Shirreff, who was highly critical of proposals regarding Scotland's military, were widely reported. 'The SNP's plans for the defence of an independent Scotland have been branded "amateurish" and "dangerous" by a former Nato commander', reported the *Express*, with the *Herald* further noting that Sir Richard had 'also said there was "no certainty" about an

DOI: 10.4324/9781003138259-4

independent Scotland, which would be seeking to rid itself of Trident nuclear weapons, becoming a member of Nato'.[1] That Scotland would have difficulties in initially joining the alliance was reported upon at various other times, such as in the following article from the *Times*: 'In words that will alarm wavering voters, Anders Fogh Rasmussen, the secretary-general [of Nato], said that any decision on accepting a new country into Nato [...] had to be unanimous among 28 member states'.[2]

Potential difficulties with membership would be frequently raised when discussing Nato, with this trend particularly evident in letters published. 'I think it certain that the US would veto any application for membership on the grounds that accepting a "paper defence force" would weaken the alliance', asserted a submission to the *Mail*, 'it would be some years before any Scottish defence force could become viable – in my view, never'.[3] Others stressed that an independent Scotland, whether a member of Nato or not, would inevitably weaken the organisation's capabilities. 'This opening of the door into the North Atlantic will not have gone unnoticed in Moscow, where Vladimir Putin has repeatedly shown willingness to embark on military adventures' threated a letter appearing in the *Telegraph*, warnings which were repeated in the *Herald*: 'An independent Scotland would weaken the UK. Scots would sit impotently between Saudi Arabia and Senegal at the UN [...] and would reduce defence expenditure when it should be increasing in all Nato countries'.[4] Similar themes would emerge in the press, with the Nato alliance and Scotland's defence prospects seen to gain extra prominence in the centre-right titles (which have an established history of reporting on the British military in glowing, often reverential, terms). 'All the indications are that membership of Nato or the European Union will be neither quick nor straightforward', commented a *Times* editorial appearing a week before the vote, 'Scotland will find itself hovering on the margins of the big alliances that give meaning and clout to small states'.[5] Echoing a contextual device which would be utilised elsewhere in the coverage, much was also made of the contemporary political landscape, with the relative volatility of 2014 regularly cited as reason to reject independence. Seeing independence as reducing Scotland's ability to effectively respond to international crises, and highlighting the UK's place as 'a permanent member of Nato, where we can exert credible political pressure on the spectrum of operations', a contribution to the *Express* questioned Scotland's potential to adapt to emerging threats: 'Will an independent Scotland deliver a credible military capability when the people express and want intervention into such conflicts as those currently experienced with ISIS?'.[6] Citing the same global instability, a letter to the *Herald* pleaded further: 'How then, in these troubled times, can we even consider independence as a viable option? [...] It's only a No vote that will protect us against anything the future may hold for us in Scotland'.[7]

There was, however, also (limited) comment which challenged the dominant narrative that Scotland would struggle to gain re-admission to Nato. For one, the aforementioned claims of Richard Shirreff would be criticised, seen in many ways as a form of baseless scaremongering. Writing for the *Scotsman*, George Kerevan was quick to dismiss the former Nato commander's warnings over Scotland's military future: 'Security is likely to be the big "scare" in the last days of a close referendum fight. Enter General Sir Richard Shirreff [...] yet another of the Oxford-educated elite who dominate the British establishment'.[8] Other contributions questioned whether membership was even desirable. For example, David Maddox, reporting on the recent Nato summit taking place in Wales, drew attention to the organisation's general lack of transparency and accommodation with the media. 'If these people are really going to claim to be the defenders of liberty, then they should be willing to be scrutinised', argued Maddox, 'This is an organisation the SNP wants an independent Scotland to join. Many Yes supporters have not been persuaded; last week would have done little to make them change their minds'.[9] Writing in the *Scotsman*, Dame Mariot Leslie, a former UK ambassador to Nato, saw Scotland's prospects in brighter terms:

> I am also in no doubt that the other 28 Nato allies would see it in their interest to welcome an independent Scotland [...] No ally would wish to interrupt the integrated Nato defence arrangements in the North Sea and North Atlantic.[10]

Emphasising an aspect which would fleetingly emerge elsewhere, other comment asserted that the issue of Nato membership should be, at the very least, the decision of an independent Scotland. 'It is the government of an independent Scotland that will decide membership of Nato or not', argued one such letter to the *Herald*, which further warned: 'In the event of a No victory membership will simply continue unchallenged, as will the status quo generally'.[11]

Inevitably, when discussing the issue of Nato membership, comment also drew attention to the contentious topic of Trident. The UK's nuclear deterrent has sharply divided opinion for decades, and press coverage of the referendum proved no exception. The role of Faslane as a major employer, what Kate Devlin termed 'the thorny issue of potentially thousands of jobs', became a regular feature of the coverage discussing Trident, with difficulties related to removal commonly invoked.[12] A *Times* feature, for example, would cite Better Together figures which argued that 'HMNB Clyde supports about 11,000 jobs and contributes £270 million a year to the local economy', though went on to add that 'Those from the Yes campaign claim that the military contribution to Helensburgh's economy is a myth'.[13] Such themes were repeated in a further report by the same title, echoing claims widely disseminated in the last weeks of August: 'Moving Trident submarines out of an independent Scotland would take at least 10 to 15 years, far longer than the Yes campaign's claims, according to one of the world's leading independent nuclear experts'.[14] Accepting the possible employment implications, Ruth Wishart nonetheless stressed the moral and ethical implications of the nuclear deterrent remaining in Scotland. 'Many of my friends and neighbours view the bases as a necessary evil [...] that is a natural instinct in a world where young people are looking for a job in an over subscribed marketplace, or one where wages from the base put food on the table', remarked such a piece in the *Herald*, 'I respect the argument but it can't take precedence over all the manifold reasons why Trident is an obscene anachronism'.[15]

Beyond practical issues of employment or relocation, among the most dominant characteristics of comment related to Trident was an apparent desire to retain the UK's nuclear deterrent. The loss of such capabilities evidently troubled several readers, with myriad letters fearful of the implications for both Scotland and the United Kingdom in the event of the Trident system being relocated. A submission to the *Scotsman* highlighted that the UK's nuclear weapons had 'been in constant use every day since they were introduced, discouraging others with nuclear weapons from trying to blackmail us, and helping to deter nuclear holocaust', going on to repeat a common refrain: 'As long as nuclear weapons exist, we are much safer having our own too'.[16] Such concerns were voiced in the *Express*, with one letter again drawing attention to what the author perceived to be a rapidly changing world:

> If Alex Salmond and his political party get rid of our Trident defence, what better defence will we have against any political enemy? Or does he believe we won't have any? [...] World issues are changing fast. We must not bury our head in the sand.[17]

A similar tone would be found in a submission to the *Mail*, which saw few reasons to be optimistic about an independent Scotland's capabilities: 'Is no one paying attention to what is happening in the world? Get rid of our nuclear deterrent? Our armed forces are much depleted, so what would we do for defence? Deploy the Brownies?'[18] A further piece, appearing the day before the vote, mixed related concerns with a rather romanticised patriotism. 'Our fluttering Saltire, the skirl of the bagpipes, the warm aroma of neeps and tatties – all are hallmarks of our unique Scottish tradition', remarked the *Herald* submission, 'But are we casting these to the wind of today's harsh realities by discarding our nuclear deterrent and reducing our defence intelligence?'[19]

Demonstrably, many interventions arguing for the retention of Trident were influenced by fears regarding an uncertain geopolitical landscape, which during this period was being vividly publicised through the actions of Islamic State. In a similar vein, the loss of Trident was also framed as potentially damaging to UK/US strategic relations. In early August, for example, official comments from across the Atlantic gained significant attention. 'Senior members of the United States Congress have stated their opposition to Scotland's potential exit from the UK, with leading figures in Washington warning a Yes vote could weaken America's "national security interest"', reported the *Scotsman*, which further contextualised the developments as 'a stark intervention amid growing concerns among the US political elite about the prospect of a vote for independence next month'.[20] Former Prime Minister John Major would cite many of these concerns, emphasising the diminished role of the United Kingdom in the event of Scottish independence: 'Trident would almost certainly be lost. Britain's role as the second largest military force in the EU would be gone and, with it, many of our close ties to the United States'.[21]

Being such an emotive issue, however, there were also many forceful arguments against the retention of Trident, with the *Herald* a regular forum for the expression of such concerns. 'The Nato nuclear defence capability will be situated in a foreign country, which is neither a member of Nato nor the EU', noted one submission, which went on to highlight potentially serious issues for the United Kingdom: 'Since the submarines will be well within Scotland's territory, Scotland will surely have the right to take over the whole command structure, and have it transported to Edinburgh'.[22] Critiquing the documentary *Scotland Votes* as 'very much an establishment view of the dangers of Scottish independence in the UK', Iain MacWhirter's column said of the broadcast: 'It avoided currency and economics and stressed Britain's diminished footprint in the world if Scotland left, ejecting Trident: rather as if Scotland's only real contribution to the UK has been as a repository for weapons of mass destruction'.[23] Ruth Wishart was also explicit in her anti-nuclear sentiments, believing Trident to be of limited utility in the face of most contemporary dangers: 'If you examine the threats and conflicts costing half the world its sleep, it's difficult to see how Trident could be used in any meaningful way'.[24] In one of the more optimistic letters to address the subject, a submission to the *Herald* pictured a potentially brighter future for Scotland:

> A country no longer providing a base for Trident nuclear submarines and warheads within its own shores [...] A country which has both the right and the confidence to play a full part in international affairs [...] Have we the confidence and courage to finally take charge of our own destiny? I fervently hope so.[25]

Perhaps somewhat predictably, the anti-Trident position appeared far more frequently in centre-left titles, with the centre-right newspapers such as the *Telegraph* or the *Express* – having established editorial positions which support the nuclear deterrent – only publishing such views in rare cases. Nonetheless, one of the more cynical interventions appeared in the *Mail*, with a letter questioning why it should take five years or more to have Trident relocated:

> For what these vessels have cost one would have thought they would be able to sail down the Clyde and out of Scottish waters in a few hours, while any weapons of mass destruction could be sent on by road the following day.[26]

Related but also separate from the Nato alliance or the complex issue of the UK's nuclear deterrent, focus was also given to discussing the impact on the general military capabilities of both Scotland and the United Kingdom, should the former choose independence. Again, the dominant theme within such coverage – especially in opinion-based contributions – was a concern over an independent Scotland being rendered less capable of defending itself. 'The fact is', opined a *Times* editorial, 'that Scotland is likely to emerge poorer, weaker, less influential and denied much of the intelligence that is currently available to the United Kingdom'.[27] Intelligence capabilities would feature regularly in discussions regarding the military, with counterterrorism appearing particularly relevant amidst the emerging and well-publicised threat of Islamic State. An editorial in the *Telegraph* argued that 'an independent Scotland will be a weaker one militarily – especially relevant in these turbulent times – less capable of the intelligence work so vital for counter-terrorism', further stating that the loss of such capabilities would 'render Scots more vulnerable to attack, but will also make Scotland an attractive back door which could allow such enemies to find their way into England and Wales'.[28] Such fears were repeated by Sir John Scarlett, the former head of the security services, in a comment piece for the *Times*. 'SIS/MI6 and our intelligence community are, of course, the work of all the nations of the United Kingdom, built up over decades, work that simply cannot be replicated in just a few years', insisted Sir John, who also invoked the spectre of a world in turmoil: 'In a complex and fast-changing world, this is a heavy responsibility. In my view the Scottish government proposals will not offer the level of protection and support currently provided by the highly sophisticated British security and intelligence agencies'.[29]

Such concerns were merely one component of a more general narrative, which argued that Scotland would be rendered less safe by choosing independence. Contemporary fears demonstrably influenced these worries, with both terrorism and Russia cited as reasons to retain the safety of the UK's combined security arrangements. A letter from Lady Jean Fforde, for example, had specific concerns regarding the safety of oil installations in the North Sea. 'Why has nobody mentioned defence? [...] It would only take one aeroplane from a terrorist organisation to blow these ships to pieces', threated the *Telegraph* submission, 'Alex Salmond's proposals for funding are largely based on tax revenue from the oil and gas industry and yet he would have no means to defend them'.[30] Though there would be occasional contributions which provided a counter-narrative, the consensus was that an independent Scotland would be isolated, under-equipped and largely defenceless.

A related aspect of such discourse was the persistent referencing of Britain's shared martial history, with this narrative anchor observed in a number of sources. Such allusions to history were revealingly selective, however; while the collective triumph of the Second World War was frequently discussed, more recent military operations in the Middle East, for example, were conspicuous by their absence. As Dan Snow would note, in launching an open letter to Scotland: 'World War Two saw English and Scottish troops fighting side by side. On D-Day, Cockneys, Scousers, Westcountrymen, boys form the valleys and Mackens were all given heart by the strains of the bagpipes'.[31] Remarking how 'we stood alone, the first nation grimly and successfully to defy the Nazi tyranny', Sir Norman Arthur continued this theme in the *Express*:

> Did we not save the world from that abomination? Do we ignore, now, how fully the blood of us all is blended in our family of four

nations, and can we ever forget how freely and willingly it flowed, as one, in those two wars?[32]

Though mentions of the Second World War were the most frequent, other references to the military history of the United Kingdom also made appearances. 'The union of England and Scotland greatly increased the security of these islands', commented a letter to the *Times*, 'and created what has been, on most counts, Europe's most successful and enduring nation [state], a bastion of freedom and security which has more than once held the pass against tyranny'.[33] History was also explicitly cited by Tom Tugendhat, addressing the apparent hypocrisy of members of the Scots Guards not having a vote in the referendum: 'This seems an odd decision for any land, but for one with such a proud military tradition as Scotland, it is positively perverse'.[34]

In the debates surrounding Nato, Trident or the military, it is notable that most opinion expressed serious concerns for the safety of an independent Scotland. Indeed, with particular emphasis in the more Unionist titles, it can be argued that an apparent 'fear of the unknown' was the common thread connecting much of this coverage. Such fears had a certain resonance during this period, which saw the crimes of 'Jihadi John' and Islamic State being among the very few stories to replace referendum coverage on front pages or in editorials. It was even reported during this time that the referendum process had blunted efforts to retaliate against Islamic State, with the vote seen to be complicating the deployment of a military response. Describing Westminster as being 'increasingly paralysed by the Scottish referendum', a *Mail* article remarked on the 'widespread suspicion that a firm announcement that Britain will join air strikes on jihadists in Iraq and Syria has been put off until after [the] vote because of fears it could fuel the Yes campaign'.[35] A letter appearing in the same title shared concerns over Islamic fundamentalism, with further fears regarding the 'global threat of ebola and other infectious diseases crossing borders' proving rather prescient:

> At this time when we need to be united against these threats, Alex Salmond wants to separate the United Kingdom [...] We are under threat from enemies foreign and domestic and need to be ready for them now. Sadly, I don't think we are.[36]

Once more, it is observed in the bulk of this coverage that the underlying narrative was a deep concern over Scotland's prospects in what was regarded as a volatile and demonstrably dangerous world. 'We shall abandon the integrated defence of UK territory, even as the world enters a dark and perilous time', noted a submission to the *Herald*, echoing such themes.[37] 'With growing international instability and a clear threat to world peace, this is clearly not the time for Scotland to break away from the United Kingdom', insisted another letter, 'Only by standing together can we play a part in the fight against extremism, injustice and deprivation'.[38]

A handful of counterarguments were presented during this period, with some contributors arguing for the benefits of Scottish independence in terms of the potential to pursue a different foreign policy from Westminster. One contribution, for example, remarked 'there is an enormous bonus in not being forced to provide cannon fodder for Westminster's wars', drawing attention to the fact that, 'Since the Union of the Crowns, Scots regiments have been cynically used with disastrous consequences [...] Iraq and Afghanistan shows the trend will continue'.[39] Others commented on the diminishing status of the United Kingdom, with one letter challenging readers to 'rid ourselves of the delusion that we exist in the last two centuries' and 'face the current century with confidence in our ability to carve our own place among other nations on the world stage'.[40] The repeated focus on the speculatively disastrous consequences of Scottish independence also generated counter opinion, with pro-independence commentators among the most explicit in their criticism of the more frightful claims. One such voice was that of George Kerevan, who challenged the assertions of Sir Richard Shirreff in his *Scotsman* column: 'If the politics of fear triumphs in this referendum it will not make us more secure in our beds'. Looking to the post-referendum period, Kerevan saw the apparent scaremongering of the No campaign as being potentially counterproductive in the longer term: 'What the politics of fear guarantees to do is poison relations between Scots and the rest of the UK, especially if we wake up still inside the Union only to find we've been duped'.[41]

Chapping on the door? Europe and beyond

Membership of the Nato alliance was not the only strategic difficulty seen to be facing Scotland, with potential negotiations with other regional and international organisations also presented in less than optimistic terms. Not least of these concerns was the issue of re-admission to the European Union (EU), with an independent Scotland's prospects of rapid reintegration regularly framed as being unlikely, at least in the short to medium term. Of course, such coverage can now be read with more than a hint of irony, given that less than two years later

Scotland (as part of the United Kingdom) would be in the process of exiting the EU, despite an overwhelming majority of Scottish voters favouring continued membership.

Consistent among such coverage was an assertion that Scotland joining the EU would be neither quick nor easy, with the comments of European leaders often cited in support of such claims. Reporting on warnings that Scotland 'would be locked out of the European Union for the best part of a decade', Graham Keeley cited the position of Spanish Prime Minister Mariano Rajoy that 'a "yes" vote would be a "torpedo to the waterline of the spirit of the European Union"'.[42] Elsewhere it was reported that Scotland 'could face a lengthy wait before it is able to secure EU membership', with a *Scotsman* article highlighting the importance to Scotland's economy of such ties: 'The issue of EU membership is seen as crucial so that Scottish firms can get access to the single market of 300 million people and be covered by EU global trade agreements'.[43] Potentially complicating Scotland's re-admission were the positions of countries such as Belgium or Spain, which themselves were dealing with the aspirations of separatist movements. 'It would be hard for a sovereign Scotland hoping to join the EU easily to gain the full support of European capitals struggling to hold their respective states together', asserted Vuk Jeremic in the *Times*, 'Scottish exceptionalism would certainly not preclude demanding entry requirements'.[44] His position would be repeated in the newspaper's editorial a few days later: 'Nor will there be a hurry to incorporate Scotland into the European Union [...] no concrete ideas have been developed as to how to overcome the objections of Spain to Scottish EU membership'.[45] Related warnings were conveyed by Steve Forbes in a guest column for the *Telegraph*, with the business giant also drawing attention to the fact that Scotland stood to lose some of the perks of remaining part of the United Kingdom. 'Scottish separatists blithely assume Scotland would join the European Union and receive all the attendant benefits. Dream on', commented Forbes, 'Even in the improbable event that Scotland were allowed in, does anyone really think it would receive rebates in the way the UK does now?'[46] The potential loss of the UK's unique EU arrangements provoked comment from other contributors, in terms somewhat ironic with the benefit of post-2016 hindsight. Catherine MacLeod would remind *Herald* readers that membership 'could take many years and there is no guarantee that the UK's hard-won opt-outs [...] will be transferred to Scotland', while John McTernan asserted there would be 'no guarantees about keeping the UK's privileged position – in fact the very opposite, no rebate, no opt-outs'.[47]

Far less frequent were contributions which saw Scotland's aspirations of EU membership more optimistically, with this angle all but ignored in the centre-right outlets. Such interventions would generally be limited to the Scottish-only newspapers, particularly the broadsheet titles of the *Herald* and *Scotsman*. In a story given scant coverage elsewhere, David Maddox would report on statements of a former President of the European Parliament: 'Ireland's Pat Cox branded opposition claims that Scotland would find itself frozen out of the EU as "sophistry" and said the country's expulsion would damage the internal market'.[48] The issue was also addressed in several letters, with a *Herald* submission highlighting the potential place of Scotland in the European project. 'The role of the EU in fostering peaceful relations between the major European powers cannot be stressed enough', opined one letter's author, further remarking upon the evident shift in the political leaning of England: 'An independent Scotland [would be] able to distance itself from the anti-European sentiments south of the Border and take the lead in adopting a constructive approach to EU membership'.[49] Appearing a week before the vote, a similar degree of prescience was revealed in another letter, which shared such concerns about the direction of the UK's political winds. 'Moreover, the negative and alarmist emphasis of Better Together [...] ignores completely the significant risks and uncertainties if Scotland should remain within the United Kingdom', the letter warned, 'not least the real possibility of a more right-wing, Europhobic Tory government after the next election'.[50] Such fears gained limited exposure in the press, however, despite ultimately being proven entirely legitimate in light of the Brexit result.

A further aspect of this discourse deserves attention, in that several commentators questioned why an independent Scotland would even have aspirations of EU membership in the first place. Such opinion, unsurprisingly, featured most heavily in those newspapers which would later support a Leave vote in the EU referendum. A letter to the *Mail*, for example, citing the 'law of unforeseen consequence', voiced concerns over Scotland's relative strength on the continent: 'No one is saying Scotland cannot go it alone, but if we vote Yes, we will be forever or until Europe absorbs us'.[51] Worries over Scotland being beholden to the whims of the EU appeared elsewhere, such as in a *Telegraph* piece by Steve Forbes which threated over the influence of Germany within the organisation. 'Another question to consider: while dealing with Westminster can be a trial, does Scotland really believe it would fare better with Berlin?', queried Forbes, 'Does tiny Scotland want to leave itself to the tender mercies of Frau Merkel and her successors?'[52]

Others critiqued the very idea of joining the EU, with some highlighting that such an aim was incompatible with the stated aims of Scottish independence. 'I can't help thinking that Alex Salmond's philosophical position is inconsistent', noted a letter appearing in the *Telegraph* on the day of the vote, which further warned against Scotland deserting the United Kingdom for Europe: '[Salmond] battles for independence and wants Scotland to have more power over its own affairs [...] The recent record of the EU is to remove powers from member nations and centralise decision-making to Brussels'.[53] In a similar vein, Quentin Letts drew attention to the apparent iconography of Salmond's choice to campaign at St Giles, noting something of a hypocrisy in the Yes campaign's stated desire to remain part of the EU. 'Mr Salmond (who has been courting hard Scots Catholic voters) was parking himself at its gates and asserting himself with symbols of a European Union often seen as a descendant of the Holy Roman Empire', opined Letts, 'It seems odd that he should embrace rule from Brussels while trying to escape the yoke of Westminster'.[54] Ultimately, EU membership was generally presented as an aspiration which, while attainable, would take Scotland years to achieve, while many other commentators saw such a goal as at odds with many aspects of independence. Given the events of 2016, where Scotland voted to remain in the EU while the United Kingdom voted narrowly to leave, it is safe to assume that this theme will remain important in continuing debates regarding independence, though coverage in the event of a second referendum may prove notably different from that observed in 2014, with the threat of losing EU membership no longer applicable in the case for remaining part of the Union.

Whether it was concerns over the loss of key alliances and trading partners, or fears regarding Scotland becoming increasingly isolated and vulnerable, the key narrative thread connecting much of this discourse was an evident uncertainty about Scotland's prospects in navigating the international stage. This would both echo and compound a similar framing of the economic future speculated to be facing an independent Scotland, the combination of which gave credence to the notion that Scotland was better off in the Union. Certainly, to paraphrase an old refrain, while no one argued that Scotland was too stupid to be independent, multiple voices were demonstrably of the opinion that the country was indeed too wee and too poor to succeed.

A key argument of this narrative – which can be read as slightly oxymoronic – was that Scotland would lose a degree of agency in becoming independent and could never hope to wield the same influence as through remaining part the United Kingdom. For whatever reason, such geostrategic concerns were raised with greater frequency in the broadsheet titles, such as in the following submission to the *Scotsman*. 'We would be a very small country, and small countries don't have the options of larger ones', stressed the letter, 'They either have to align themselves to the defence policies of big friends or take the buffeting and blasts of unkind winds in a dangerous, volatile world'.[55] The loss of Scotland's place (as part of the United Kingdom) on the UN Security Council also drew comment, with various writers arguing that an independent Scotland would have less clout on the world stage. As a *Times* editorial insisted, once again linking such fears to contemporary issues: 'A future Scotland may well disapprove of the jihadist threat from Iraq and Syria but will be powerless to act against it unless the Kremlin gives it approval'.[56] Scotland would be 'weaker not stronger, a tiny isolated nation rather than a part of a world power', lamented another contribution, while Vuk Jeremic emphasised that, 'For the first time in modern history, Edinburgh would be directly subject to the ebbs and flows of geo-strategic circumstances'.[57] Such discussions also saw independence as having serious implications beyond the borders of Britain, with the dissolution of the UK's collective security apparatus and institutional placing being regarded as having the potential to exert pressures on the wider political landscape. 'Our stabilising influence would be eroded, sending further tremors through an already volatile world', worried Tom Tugendhat, while a *Telegraph* comment piece framed the vote as having global significance: 'It is no exaggeration to say that [independence] will fundamentally affect the course of Europe and, indeed, Western civilization'.[58] A handful of contributions challenged this dominant narrative, though remained vastly outweighed by the content arguing for Scotland to remain part of the United Kingdom. One submission gently critiqued the 'too wee' aspect of the discourse, highlighting that the 'outgoing head of Nato is Danish and the incoming one is Norwegian'.[59] In a more cynical tone, the issue was raised in a letter to the *Mail*, which saw Scotland as wielding little influence in arrangements as they stood with the United Kingdom: 'One of the fallacies put about by the No campaign is that Scotland would have less influence in the world as an independent country, but as the song goes How Can You Lose What You've Never Owned?'[60]

Much was also made of what the United Kingdom stood to lose in the event of independence, with the prestige and influence of the country both expected to suffer. 'If Great Britain, which is still seen as the epicentre of democracy and the rule of law, can't hold itself together', worried Steve Forbes, 'then the message will be that no one can'.[61]

Jenni Russell would cite similar concerns, evidently fearful of the societal or ideological ramifications resulting from Scotland gaining independence: 'It's the liberal values we live by that are under threat. If we don't take care to defend and argue for them, they may soon be the past'.[62] An anonymous submission to the *Mail* went further than most, arguing that a Yes vote would 'create conditions for conflict. If you don't believe that look at Ukraine and the Middle East'. The letter continued, 'Don't think that could happen here? Think again. History prior to the Union demonstrates how easily this can happen'.[63] Related contributions would also remark, though infrequently, on the fact that the UK's enemies were apparently rather satisfied with the ongoing uncertainty facing the country, with a piece in the *Mail* revealing that Scottish independence was both desired and feared by a range of international actors: 'With barely concealed glee and horrified fascination, world leaders who generally maintain only a tenuous relationship with the democratic process are training their eyes on the independence referendum this week'.[64]

Once again, allusions to the UK's history – particularly its military component – were cited in various contributions, with those explicitly arguing for a No vote regularly invoking this aspect in discussions about foreign policy. A letter in the *Scotsman* threatened that a 'probable and regrettable outcome of a Yes majority vote [...] will be increased pressure for the diminished UK [...] to lose its seat on the UN Security Council', a position which the submission commented had been 'justly earned by UK actions in the Second World War'.[65] A similar contribution, though questionable in its grasp of history, asserted the author's 'Pride in defending freedom in two world wars when we stood alone in the second and eventually won with the aid of the US and USSR who came in late', going on to emphasise Britain's legacy in the world: 'Our Union has been, in global terms, the finest of all in propagating civilized values'.[66] Further commentary raised concerns over a loss of important connections, should Scotland achieve independence. 'Does Scotland really want to press the self-destruct button?', argued a letter to the *Herald*, 'We are treated with respect worldwide in our important role as part of the UK, but is it not selfish and self-defeating to push Scots towards separation?'[67] Such sentiments would be repeated in the *Mail*, with one contribution reminding readers that the United Kingdom remained 'a nation respected and listened to throughout the world'; while a *Scotsman* piece, focusing on the UK's established defence arrangements, lamented, 'Why on earth would we want to throw that away?'[68]

Road to nowhere? The presentation of an uncertain future

Taken together, the bulk of coverage observed in relation to policy issues, whether they be economic or strategic, shared a distinct similarity; in that the prospects of an independent Scotland were generally framed as being challenging at best, and disastrous at worst. Uncertainty regarding an independent Scotland's future – over policy aspects such as currency, oil resources, trading arrangements, membership of international organisations or defence considerations – was a persistent aspect of the discourse, with examples appearing in various sources. Though the potential for an independent Scotland to succeed was at times entertained as a concept, particularly in the Scottish titles examined, the balance of the discourse was generally negative, with this being especially pronounced in the centre-right titles. With emerging and ongoing issues facing both Scotland the international community, not least the societal and economic impact of the coronavirus pandemic, it is highly likely that moving forward the framing of Scottish independence will continue to rely heavily on a narrative which stresses the unpredictable and volatile nature of the global political landscape. Indeed, somewhat ironically, should the question of independence be put to the Scottish people once more, one thing that can be predicted with a degree of certainty is that the concept of uncertainty will again be emphasised by the press.

Notes

1 David Scott, "Nato general rubbishes SNP as 'amateurish on defence'", *Express*, 1.9.14, p. 5; Michael Settle & Kate Devlin, "Former Nato chief calls SNP plans amateurish", *Herald*, 1.9.14, p. 7.
2 Deborah Haynes, "Scotland is told: you'll have to join Nato queue", *Times*, 19.8.14, p. 1.
3 Donald McKenzie, "Defend our defence", *Mail*, 5.9.14, p. 60.
4 Clive Kent, "The independence campaign has betrayed Scotland's proud identity", *Telegraph*, 18.9.14, p. 21; James Pickett, "Our security demands that the UK should be an effective force", *Herald*, 12.9.14, p. 21.
5 Editorial, "Limbo-land", *Times*, 11.9.14, p. 34.
6 Ian Smith, "Sticking together will be the best defence", *Express*, 29.8.14, p. 50.
7 Grant Ker, "The scale of potential job losses at Faslane has been greatly underestimated", *Herald*, 17.9.14, p. 20.
8 George Kerevan, "Going over the top about defences", *Scotsman*, 3.9.14, p. 25.
9 David Maddox, "Inside Westminster", *Scotsman*, 9.9.14, p. 23.
10 Dame Mariot Leslie, "Nato not an issue for a solo Scotland", *Scotsman*, 3.9.14, p. 32.
11 Brian Quail, "Scots women are not voting No out of a sense of timidity", *Herald*, 14.8.14, p. 14.
12 Kate Devlin, "The big question: Defence", *Herald*, 29.8.14, p. 6.

13 Katie Gibbons, "This is a garrison town – losing Faslane will be devastating for it", *Times*, 12.9.14, p. 8.
14 Scotland Staff, "Trident removal date 'impossible'", *Times*, 22.8.14, p. 15.
15 Ruth Wishart, "Case for removing obscene anachronism that is Trident", *Herald*, 15.8.14, p. 15.
16 Ian Gardner, "Why throw away our defence security?", *Scotsman*, 9.9.14, p. 26.
17 David McNeill, "We need unity to face changing global threat", *Express*, 29.8.14, p. 50.
18 C Webster, "What a deterrent!", *Mail*, 4.9.14, p. 56.
19 Gavin Steven, "The scale of potential job losses at Faslane has been greatly underestimated", *Herald*, 17.9.14, p. 20.
20 Andrew Whitaker, "US politicians backing UK's own 'special relationship'", *Scotsman*, 8.8.14, p. 8.
21 John Major, "Labour's deadly legacy puts the Union at risk", *Times*, 10.9.14, p. 25.
22 EL Lloyd, "It is folly to cling on to the delusion that the United Kingdom is still a great power", *Herald*, 11.9.14, p. 16.
23 Iain MacWhirter, "Time to stop opprobrium that is heaped on Scotland", *Herald*, 14.8.14, p. 13.
24 Wishart, "Case for removing".
25 Iain Mann, "The English are not as engaged in our debate as they should be", *Herald*, 18.8.14, p. 14.
26 John Eoin Douglas, "Road trip bombshell", *Mail*, 29.8.14, p. 60.
27 Editorial, "Limbo-land".
28 Editorial, "A glimmer of hope", *Telegraph*, 15.9.14, p. 21.
29 Sir John Scarlett, "A Yes vote brings grave security dangers", *Times*, 5.9.14, p. 32.
30 Lady Jean Fforde, "Defending Scotland", *Telegraph*, 1.9.14, p. 17.
31 Dan Snow, "Disunited Kingdom", *Sun*, 3.9.14, p. 10.
32 Sir Norman Arthur, "Don't throw away a shared history to be proud of", *Express*, 9.9.14, p. 12.
33 Robert Page, "Scotland between the high road and the low", *Times*, 19.8.14, p. 29.
34 Tom Tugendhat, "Soldiers with no say in the country they defend", *Telegraph*, 29.8.14, p. 19.
35 James Chapman & Alan Roden, "Attacks on jihadis 'being delayed for fear of handing a boost to Yes vote'", *Mail*, 10.9.14, p. 7.
36 Shaun O'Hare, "Foes should bind us", *Mail*, 9.9.14, p. 56.
37 Robert Paris, "Whatever the outcome, we can be confident Scots will do their best to heal society", *Herald*, 11.9.14, p. 17.
38 W Finlday, "It is folly to cling to the delusion that the United Kingdom is still a great power", *Herald*, 11.9.14, p. 16.
39 Charlie Pollock, "Positive case for voting No lies in being proud of what we have", *Herald*, 1.9.14, p. 14.
40 KM Campbell, "It is folly to cling to the delusion that the United Kingdom is still a great power", *Herald*, 11.9.14, p. 16.
41 Kerevan, "Going over the top about defences".
42 Graham Keeley, "You'll be shut out of EU for years, Spanish PM says in 'torpedo alert'", *Times*, 18.9.14, p. 10.

43 Scott MacNab, "Salmond: Talks have started on Scotland joining the EU", *Scotsman*, 15.9.14, p. 4.

44 Vuk Jeremic, "It may be hard to find allies outside the Union", *Times*, 9.9.14, p. 29.

45 Editorial, "Limbo-land".

46 Steve Forbes, "He'll never be a big player", *Telegraph*, 17.9.14, p. 23.

47 Catherine MacLeod, "Scotland needs the UK's broad shoulders", *Herald*, 18.9.14, p. 19; John McTernan, "Facts are as fatal to the SNP as garlic is to a vampire", *Mail*, 9.9.14, p. 14.

48 Scott MacNab, "Scotland would join EU within 18 months", *Scotsman*, 9.9.14, p. 4.

49 Willie Maclean, "Positive case for voting No lies in being proud of what we have", *Herald*, 1.9.14, p. 14.

50 Norman Shanks, "The shoogly peg brigade", *Herald*, 11.9.14, p. 16.

51 Garret Croner, "Proud shared history", *Mail*, 1.9.14, p. 54.

52 Forbes, "He'll never be a big player".

53 Mick Ferrie, "The independence campaign has betrayed Scotland's proud identity", *Telegraph*, 18.9.14, p. 27.

54 Quentin Letts, "The Salmondistas cried 'Yes' – in nine different languages", *Mail*, 10.9.14, p. 8.

55 Gardner, "Why throw away our defence security?".

56 Editorial, "Limbo-land".

57 Peter Hain, "Mr Salmond, you're no Nelson Mandela – Scotland is free already", *Telegraph*, 12.9.14, p. 24; Jeremic, "It may be hard".

58 Tugendhat, "Soldiers with no say in the country they defend"; Forbes, "He'll never be".

59 Eva Tyson, "Power brokers", *Scotsman*, 16.9.14, p. 26.

60 Eddie Laughlan, "Nothing to lose", *Mail*, 16.9.14, p. 62.

61 Forbes, "He'll never be".

62 Jenni Russell, "Scottish anger reflects a world breaking apart", *Times*, 18.9.14, p. 30.

63 Name and address supplied, "Grim lessons", *Mail*, 8.8.14, p. 54.

64 Will Pavia, "Axis of Alex: rogues gallery of world leaders look to new ally", *Times*, 16.9.14, p. 8.

65 John Birkett, "Do we benefit from UK foreign policy?", *Scotsman*, 4.9.14, p. 28.

66 William Scott, "Positive case for voting No lies in being proud of what we have", *Herald*, 1.9.14, p. 14.

67 Joy Williamson, "Whatever the outcome, we can be confident Scots will do their best to heal society", *Herald*, 11.9.14, p. 17.

68 Margaret Mitchell, "Union worth preserving", *Mail*, 9.9.14, p. 56; Gardner, "Why throw away".

5 Everyone's got an opinion

Celebrities, royalty and the Conservative Party

Coverage of the referendum, of course, often focused on policies, themes and issues, but a huge proportion of press engagement with the independence debate took individuals as the focal point of reporting. In a celebrity-obsessed world, where party politics are often personified through reference to a few key individuals in each party, it was inevitable that the views of various elites would be highlighted and discussed in such a manner. What is perhaps most telling though is the observation that interventions from such individuals were framed in vastly different ways, depending on both the person in question and the political position they were endorsing.

The great and the good

Though celebrities figured in the coverage only fleetingly, they tended to gain prominent placing and publicity on the occasions where they did intervene.[1] Such public pronouncements could invoke the ire of those with opposing positions on independence, and the online reaction to celebrity-backed comments often drew further attention from the press. For example, the *Scotsman* reported that police had 'warned social media users over their conduct after "vile and disgusting" comments were posted about tennis star Andy Murray', while the *Express* took a different angle on Murray's late endorsement of a Yes vote: 'Andy Murray yesterday admitted he made a mistake over the way he declared his support for independence'.[2] Other celebrity interventions bordered on the surreal, at least in relation to the short-lived media exposure their political opinions would generate. Perhaps the most notable example of this phenomenon was the front page coverage devoted to comments from football commentator, Archie Macpherson. 'Voice of football Archie Macpherson upstaged the politicians yesterday as he made an impassioned plea to keep Britain together', announced

DOI: 10.4324/9781003138259-5

David Clegg of the *Record*, 'The commentator – famous for exclaiming "woof!" – made an electrifying speech at a Better Together event'.[3] MacPherson's speech was also praised by Lindsay McIntosh of the *Times*, who noted of those in attendance: 'For some in the audience, whose childhood Saturdays were punctuated by his catchphrases, he stole the show'.[4] Despite the questionable relevance of the speaker to Scotland's greatest constitutional question for three centuries, further broadsheet coverage would follow, with Magnus Gardham noting (in another front page article) how Macpherson had 'emerged as the No campaign's surprise weapon' and had 'turned his talents to politics [...] with a barnstorming speech'.[5]

By far the most concerted effort to bring celebrities into the referendum debate came with the publication of a 'love letter' to Scotland, first conceived of by broadcaster Dan Snow. The Let's Stay Together campaign was a collaborative effort by Snow and Tom Holland which gathered signatures from a variety of celebrities wishing to express their desire for Scotland to vote No, with the likes of Ross Kemp and Sir Steve Redgrave among those lending their endorsement. The tabloid press, as expected, ran with the celebrity-centric story, with a double-page spread in the *Sun* leading with the fact that Bruce Forsyth had thrown 'his weight behind a celebrity campaign to keep Scotland part of the UK', further noting that the letter had 'already drawn support from Eddie Izzard and Tony Robinson'.[6] Such coverage was not restricted to the tabloids, however. 'The awards amassed by the signatories include 18 Olympic gold medals, 44 Bafta awards, one Nobel Prize and two Turner prizes', noted the *Telegraph*, highlighting that the letter's organisers hoped it would be 'seen in Scotland as an appeal by the rest of the UK not to leave the Union'.[7] Indeed, the *Telegraph* went one further, granting Holland a guest comment piece, where he explained the reasoning behind the campaign:

> I hope that any Scots uncertain whether or not there is affection and admiration for them in the rest of the UK will look at our letter and find, in the sheer range and heft of its signatories, the decisive answer.[8]

The campaign even generated a degree of positive editorial coverage, the section of the newspaper usually devoted to the most pressing issues of the day. An *Express* editorial opined that the 'plea for Britain to stick together is hugely welcome and shows that the independence issue has now gripped the whole of the UK', somewhat patronisingly going on to offer the following: 'If you have still to make up your mind, the list is very long and contains people from every way of life. Hopefully it will tip a few more towards a No vote'.[9]

This specific intervention, as was perhaps expected, also provoked both critique and ridicule. The words of *Sun* columnist Bill Leckie reflected this widespread rejection of such celebrity endorsements: 'I mean, Bruce bloody Forsyth. A 276-year-old man who spends half his time living in Puerto Rico and who has as much relevance to Scotland's future as Alex Salmond has to ballroom dancing'.[10] Focusing on the introduction of the same celebrity, the *Record* published an editorial questioning the wisdom of the Better Together campaign. 'Now we're told Bruce Forsyth is a secret weapon to save the Union', stated the lead article, 'How ludicrous, patronising, insulting and self-defeating. What exactly was the message the organisers were hoping to send? Nice to rule you, to rule you, nice?'[11] Letters pages also attracted comment on this aspect of the campaign. One such contribution to the *Mail* would assert, 'The final insult was the "love letter" urging us to stay in the Union from well-off celebrities who will never suffer under a Tory government', with a submission to the *Sun* questioning, 'Why does this unending litany of "stars" – the majority of whom are not Scottish – feel they have the right to tell the Scots not to leave the Union?'[12] Evidently, though interventions from celebrity figures indeed garnered publicity within the press, their overall impact may not have been as originally intended, with many in the media actively mocking this particular effort.

The view from Buckingham Palace

With celebrities like Mick Jagger gaining prominent coverage simply for having an opinion on the independence debate, it is unsurprising that the views of the Royals would also command significant attention – with the guarded remarks of the Queen, in particular, prompting a remarkable number of articles and comment pieces. Though there were brief and infrequent mentions of other members of the House of Windsor, with one imaginative example proposing that Princess Anne be made Queen of Scotland, for all intents and purposes the only Royal personality who mattered in the independence debate was the reigning monarch.[13] In what would become a focal point of reporting during the campaign, though later revealed as one of the most stage-managed aspects of it, the Queen's only public utterance on the referendum first appeared in the press on 15 September. Reported by the *Mail* to be 'an extraordinary plea for caution in the referendum yesterday in the strongest indication yet that the Monarch longs for Scotland to remain part of the United Kingdom', it was described how the Queen had approached well-wishers at Crathie Kirk and, prompted by a question from a member of the public, stated: 'I hope everybody thinks very carefully about the referendum this week'.[14] Of this particular interaction, Peter Hennessy would later assert, 'any biography of her will now linger on the Crathie moment [...] the photo of her about to chat to well-wishers and how niftily and technically neutrally it was done'.[15]

That the Queen should have addressed her subjects in such a manner was in itself a highly unusual occurrence, with the press quick to stress how atypical the interaction had been. 'It is all but unheard of for the Queen to do a walkabout at Crathie Kirk', noted the *Mail*, adding that the monarch 'considers Sunday service there to be her own private act of worship rather than a public ceremony'.[16] The remark attracted front page coverage from various outlets, with the *Telegraph* devoting considerable attention to the Queen's words and how she had 'broke with protocol and spoke with well-wishers outside the church', further contextualising her utterance by noting that the Royal family had attended a service 'that had included a prayer asking God "to save us from false choices"'.[17] Other coverage continued to highlight the unprecedented nature of the Queen's intervention, while also observing that aspects of the interaction had been choreographed and ultimately undertaken for the benefit of the media. As Gordon Rayner remarked: 'Equally unusual was the curiously accommodating behaviour of the police sergeant on duty at Crathie, who invited the press to get close enough to record the moment'.[18] Torcuil Crichton of the *Record* provided additional comment on this aspect, describing the event as 'what appeared to be a deliberately timed and veiled message', adding that, 'the Queen made sure reporters were present when she spoke'.[19]

Although the Queen's message had been carefully worded so as not to explicitly endorse a position in the referendum, the press were not long in speculating on the meaning of her words. Particularly prevalent in the centre-right titles, much of the coverage following the Queen's comments went on to emphasise that the supposedly neutral statement had in fact been an endorsement of the Union. 'Although the Queen's words do not directly express a view', wrote Lindsay McIntosh, 'they will be interpreted by some on the No side as a plea to Scots not to base their decision on fleeting arguments'.[20] A *Telegraph* report, noting the 'hugely significant intervention', would claim that the statement was 'being viewed last night as the clearest sign yet that she hopes for a No vote on Thursday', while a *Mail* article highlighted the degree to which the Queen's words had been welcomed by many: 'Her remark – widely seen as a counsel of caution over independence – electrified the debate and was privately greeted with delight in the No camp'.[21] Predictably, for a title which gives regular and positive coverage to the monarchy, the *Mail* was evidently eager to translate the meaning of the Queen's words. A front page article, utilising the exact phrasing of the *Telegraph*'s interpretation, noted how 'her remarks were widely seen as a counsel of caution over independence', adding that 'the fact she went out of her way to address the issue [...] was seen as carefully choreographed and highly symbolic'.[22] The *Mail* would further report on the general reaction to the Queen's intervention, highlighting that 'Pro-Union MPs applauded her call to think "carefully" about how they vote', before again arguing that many had interpreted her words 'as clear support for keeping Scotland in the UK'.[23]

The *Sun* took a slightly less interpretive perspective, addressing the intervention in its editorial column in a manner which praised the monarch while also refusing to necessarily divine a stance from her words:

> If someone urges you to think carefully about buying a house or a car, it's not the same as telling you what decision to make [...] It is unarguable that the United Kingdom means everything to HM, but that also means she will treat the free will of her subjects with just as much respect.[24]

A related example appeared in the *Herald*, which highlighted that 'neither side in the campaign [had] tried to capitalise on the remarks'.[25] This final point is debatable, as it could reasonably be argued that the general tone of the coverage had been shaped to fit the aims of the No campaign, which by this point had well-established connections with the more conservative-leaning press, in particular. In other words, the Queen's statement may indeed have been technically neutral and her words had not been explicitly cited or endorsed by either official campaign, but both of these factors were arguably negated by a compliant and reverential press, which propagated the words of the exchange in a manner which was conceivably beneficial to only one side of the debate. Certainly, a *Telegraph* piece was fairly accurate in observing how the statement bore, 'all the hallmarks of a premeditated piece of media management by Her Majesty to plead with Scots to stay in the Union'. As the same article would note, 'The Queen simply does not make such comments by accident [...] what other conclusion are we to draw than that she is concerned the Scots will take a rash step into the unknown by voting Yes?'[26]

The Queen's remarks did not appear in a vacuum, however, emerging instead at the end of a week where numerous outlets had already been speculating on her feelings regarding the vote. Several days before the Crathie comments, it was reported that talks had been held with David Cameron, 'as fears grew in Buckingham Palace that Scotland could vote to go it alone'.[27] The *Telegraph* also drew attention to the fact that the Prime Minister was 'under growing pressure to ask the Queen to speak out in support of the Union', revealing that 'Senior MPs [had] suggested an intervention from Her Majesty could "make all the difference"'.[28] Even before the Queen had said anything at all on the matter, multiple news and comment pieces spoke to her supposed true feelings on the debate. As argued by a *Telegraph* editorial: 'Her Majesty, currently in residence in Balmoral, can only be watching this unfolding calamity with the same trepidation as millions of her subjects'.[29] This was echoed in the *Express*, with a report revealing that the Queen was '"horrified" over the possibility of Scottish independence', while the *Record* noted that the 'spectre of a Yes vote' had 'dominated discussions between the Queen and the PM at Balmoral'.[30] It was also publicised in the days preceding the Queen's words that 'there was a "great deal of concern" among the royal family at the prospect of a win for the Yes campaign', with Peter McKay commenting on the historical juncture at which the Prime Minister and the Head of State now found themselves: 'After half a century of modern Scottish Nationalism [...] the Queen and Cameron find themselves the monarch and PM who are most likely to face a ScotNat victory and its unknown consequences'.[31]

Theorising on the Queen's position oscillated in tone between the explicit and the guarded, but virtually all such coverage was in agreement that the Queen had, in not so many words, heartily endorsed the Union. This should come as little surprise as several newspapers, in addition to wondering if and when some form of Royal intervention would materialise, spent the days leading to her comments emphasising what Scotland meant to the Queen on a personal level. 'Talk to anyone who knows the Queen well and they will testify to her love of Scotland', wrote Robert Hardman, 'It's not just a love of pipes and scenery and cosy familiarity. It's a passionate sense of belonging'.[32] Similarly emotive language was utilised by Allison Pearson, who argued that the Queen had 'loved Scotland before she fully understood who and what she was', going on to warn: 'The Queen has no need to make the case for the Union. She *is* the Union. To dismantle it is to deal her an irreparable blow'.[33] Other coverage, remaining somewhat sycophantic in their praise of the monarch, sought to draw attention to the duration and nature of her reign. Hardman noted how she had 'presided over several separatist punch-ups during her 62-year reign', with Peter Oborne (writing days before the Crathie remarks) combining praise with a concern that she might have been expected to do more:

> The Queen has reigned marvellously for more than 60 years, and it is most unfair that she has been faced, at the age of 88, with the most important decision of her reign. But if everything goes wrong next week, how she will regret not having done more to fight for Great Britain.[34]

Fearing the worst, an *Express* piece commented further on the Queen's age, arguing that she should not be expected to deal with whatever political and constitutional issues arose in the event of a Yes vote. 'The Queen is too majestic to take part in such a travesty', opined Michael Cole, 'If the reality of a separate Scotland dawns, the Queen may decide that she had done her bit. At the age of 88, no one could blame her'.[35]

A telling component of this coverage, which reveals much about the selective reverence given to the words of the monarch, was the later backlash against David Cameron for inadvertently revealing the Queen's true feelings on the matter. Though the press had generally taken the Queen's words and explicitly interpreted them as being a defence of the Union – on the back of several days of speculation regarding the Queen's opinion and in some cases advocating a stronger intervention – the Prime Minister's revelation that the monarch had '"purred" with relief' upon hearing the result brought a fair degree of criticism.[36] Described as 'an extraordinary breach of protocol', Cameron's comments to Michael Bloomberg – picked up on microphone – were said to have forced an 'apology to the monarch [...] thought to be without precedent for a serving premier'.[37] The error for which Cameron was adjudged to have been guilty was explicitly revealing the Queen's political position, despite the fact that many in the press had already done something very similar just a few weeks prior. As John MacLeod opined in the *Mail*, 'perhaps most grave, a Queen who is meant to be above party and faction, politics and politicians has now had her private opinions on an extraordinarily emotive constitutional and civic issue laid bare and beyond doubt'.[38]

This latter point is perhaps the most crucial aspect regarding coverage of the Queen's words, given the established principal that the monarch is not supposed to intervene explicitly in political matters.

Knowing this to be the case, the supposed impartiality of the Queen was therefore stressed at almost every available opportunity, both in the days before and in the period after the comments made outside Crathie Kirk. The issue of the Queen's neutrality was discussed in virtually every instance of press engagement with the monarch's stance on Scottish independence, with some reports seeking to stress the efforts being made to keep the Queen detached from the debate altogether. Michael Cole described the 'strenuous efforts to keep the Queen out of the political maelstrom created by this dangerous referendum', with a *Times* article revealing that Buckingham Palace had 'taken the unprecedented step of warning politicians not to drag the Queen into the battle over Scottish independence', drawing attention to 'unusually forceful language betraying signs of irritation at the highest level'.[39] Other sources were at pains to emphasise reports that the Queen would 'maintain a neutral stance', thus framing her statement in terms which apparently observed certain protocols and expectations surrounding such interventions.[40] 'Royal aides have stressed the Queen's neutrality in the debate, believing independence is a matter for the Scottish people', observed a *Herald* front page article, 'The Queen, who remains above the political fray as a constitutional monarch, observed the proprieties of not endorsing either side in the referendum'.[41] That the Queen's impartiality would be an issue worth consideration by the media drew explicit comment from some quarters, as highlighted by Gordon Rayner: 'Her press secretaries tried their best to spin the comment as proof of her neutrality, and repeated the mantra that "the Queen regards the referendum as entirely a matter for the Scottish people"'.[42]

A revealing dynamic in relation to the Queen's position on independence was a changing debate about the constitutional limitations placed on her position. In the days prior to her utterance, several commentators confidently announced that the monarch would remain strictly tight-lipped about the whole affair, with Robert Hardman asserting there was 'not the remotest chance that the Queen will voice any sort of opinion'.[43] Others stated that such an intervention was all but impossible, due to the ill-feeling it could potentially unleash: 'Imagine the uproar and threat to the monarchy's existence if she abandoned a reign-long discipline of not interfering in politics and advised Scots not to support the Nationalists'.[44] Even as her comments were being directly quoted, coverage would reassert that the Queen remained impartial. 'Buckingham Palace has repeatedly insisted the Queen is "above politics"', stated a *Mail* article, simultaneously drawing attention to the fact that observers had 'pointed out that her appearance with her two most senior heirs seemed to be a carefully choreographed show of unity in Scotland ahead of Thursday's referendum'.[45]

Indicative of the importance placed on the referendum's outcome, however, were the number of contributors who actively advocated *for* the Queen to break with protocol in order to help preserve the Union. In part, such demands emanated from a belief that politicians had thus far done a less than satisfactory job in promoting the case for the United Kingdom: 'In the absence of guidance from a much-loved Head of State we are reliant upon last-ditch political manoeuvring to save the Union'. The same editorial would continue, 'It is a long-standing convention, scrupulously observed by the Queen, that she should maintain a neutral position in all political controversies', before concluding, 'Yet when the future of the country is at stake it is at least questionable whether the same protocols apply'.[46] That the Queen should be more involved in the defence of the Union prompted much discussion, gaining particular traction in the *Telegraph* and *Mail*. 'It is true that she has always understood the importance of remaining neutral and above politics', noted Peter Oborne, before arguing, 'this vote is not about party politics. It is about the survival of the British state'.[47] Gordon Rayner echoed such sentiments, though was more direct in his opinion: 'For a Head of State, speaking in defence of their country is not party politics. It is a right and, some would say, a duty'.[48] Perhaps the most pleading commentary in this regard came from Stephen Glover, in a comment piece for the *Mail*. Berating the efforts of the mainstream politicians, he argued that 'the Queen could still rescue us, if only she were allowed to by the timid people surrounding her'. Accepting the constitutional predicament of such a direct intervention, Glover stood firm in his desire to see the monarch come out explicitly for the Unionist cause:

> Of course, there would be risks to the Queen's position, but we face a national crisis so grave that those who revere Her Majesty should put the constitutional rulebook to one side, and ask her to make a sacrifice for the country she loves, and has served so magnificently.[49]

For something which was barely a dozen words, the remarks of the Queen generated a remarkable degree of coverage. Whether this is evidence that the monarch has direct influence in political affairs is undetermined, but the manner of the intervention reveals much about the reverence and cultural capital which the Queen, if not necessarily the wider monarchy, is seen to enjoy. Though few could explicitly agree on what had (or had not) been said, the fact that the Queen had made any comment at all was newsworthy in itself. It would of course later be revealed that the entire event had been highly stage-managed, and partly at the behest of David Cameron, yet the attention which the issue was afforded speaks volumes about the manner in which the opinions of certain elites were granted privileged status in terms of how their words were propagated during the referendum campaign. Few come more elite than the Queen, and her words were dissected, interpreted and speculated upon ad nauseam. Constitutional considerations essentially forbid the monarch from making a direct statement, but a generally compliant media took it upon themselves (as surely was anticipated) to fill in the blanks and thus present the Queen's position as one which supported the Union, while still insisting that she remained above the political fray.

Tears of a Tory: David Cameron and the Conservative Party

The senior partner in the coalition government in 2014, the Conservative Party were sure to feature in the coverage of the referendum debate. Their general unpopularity in Scotland, however, meant that even their most recognised politicians were often kept at arm's length, at least in terms of being the focus of major press coverage. Boris Johnson, for example, appeared only fleetingly in the coverage, despite his well-established fondness for media appearances, with one such story highlighting that he had 'provoked anger among independence campaigners by claiming that there was "no need" to devolve more powers over taxation to Holyrood'.[50] The future Prime Minister did submit a piece for the *Telegraph* though, addressing the issue of independence in typically dramatic language: 'I mean that we will be zombies, walking dead, because a fundamental part of our identity will have been killed. We will all have lost a way of thinking about ourselves, a way of explaining ourselves to the world'.[51] Other luminaries of the party, such as William Hague or John Major, figured in the form of comment pieces, but their input was deliberately minimised, and generally restricted to newspapers which supported the Tories. Indeed, Theresa May, who would go on to succeed David Cameron as Prime Minister in 2016, would be all but invisible in the coverage, a notable observation, given that she would hold the highest office of the United Kingdom less than two years after the state was in serious jeopardy. Again, it is likely that the dearth of official Conservative voices in much of the coverage was a deliberate campaign tactic, with an historically unpopular party leading the campaign to save the Union more than likely to backfire. Commenting on the lack of a solid electoral base for the Tories in Scotland, Alex Massie would write:

> Each year fresh expeditions venture out in search of Tory Scotti-cus, attempting to find the last remaining members of the tribe [...] perhaps conditions one day will allow their fortunes to recover. Like beavers – or even wolves – perhaps they can be reintroduced to Scotland.[52]

Much has been made in the period since the referendum regarding Ruth Davidson's role during the campaign, with some seeing her as a key and determining voice in the eventual No victory. While it is true that Davidson can be credited, in some part, with the improvement of the Scottish Tories' electoral fortunes – illustrated most clearly in the 2017 general election results – that she was indeed a main player in the No campaign is a position which, though subsequently entrenched in the narrative, does not survive close scrutiny. Davidson certainly made a number of campaign appearances in the run-up to the vote, but in terms of being a focal point of the press coverage, her influence was generally restricted to photo-ops and frequent 'response' quotes seeking to challenge some aspect of the Yes campaign.[53] Nonetheless, the positioning of Ruth Davidson as a hard-working and effective champion of the Union started almost immediately after the vote was sealed. Her speech at the Conservative Party conference was heralded for gaining 'two standing ovations', with it further noted that David Cameron had attended Davidson's speech and 'raised one hand and given her a thumbs-up at the conclusion'.[54] Indeed, even the *Record*, a newspaper typically hostile to the Conservatives, provided positive coverage of her conference appearance, and to the response her re-marks had generated from the audience in attendance.[55] To reiterate, however, when judged purely on the relative attention afforded her campaigning and statements, Ruth Davidson was, contrary to what has become something of an established fact, not an integral part of delivering the No campaign's message through the newspaper medium in 2014.

The one prominent Conservative given, on occasion, the full focus of the press was, of course, David Cameron. Certainly, the Prime Minister of the United Kingdom – the political entity in jeopardy of ceasing to exist – would be expected to have at least some opinion on the matter of the referendum. The main interventions of the Prime Minister, how-ever, came late in the process, and were largely stage-managed affairs.

Despite being the leader of the United Kingdom, Cameron remained a Tory and the Better Together campaign was well aware of how poorly his style and political affiliations could play with a Scottish audience. Overall, the coverage of Cameron's statements or speeches was generally positive, with his commitment to retaining the Union often highlighted in the text. As Mike Settle asserted: 'he is, where the Union is concerned, a conviction politician: he really does believe in the United Kingdom'.[56] The *Sun*, less Tory-supporting than its English edition, also gave Cameron a degree of praise, saying of a speech in Scotland's capital: 'Let's give some credit where credit is due – David Cameron gave a wonderful performance in Edinburgh yesterday'. The Andrew Nicoll piece further noted that the Prime Minister had been 'calm, assured, relaxed and genuinely passionate about the United Kingdom – the country he loves with a true, undisguised patriotism'.[57]

Taking something of a backseat in the debate, at least until the final fortnight, Cameron was also cited as being an intelligent political operator, cognizant of his own apparent political weaknesses. As Andrew Pierce opined in the *Mail*: 'But with only one MP in Scotland, Cameron was painfully aware that his brand of Old Etonian Toryism is toxic north of the Border'.[58] The Prime Minister's political savvy also drew comment in relation to his refusal to directly debate the independence issue, after Alex Salmond 'threw down the gauntlet for a telly showdown'.[59] Of the unlikely prospects of such a face-off, a *Sun* editorial remarked, 'Mr Cameron might be a lot of things, but daft is not one of them. He knows exactly how his very English, public schoolboy tones would play to a Scottish audience'. Speculating on the optics and probable outcome of such a debate, the article continued:

> Posh Tory boy against Wee Eck giving it his breast-beating, tub-thumping Braveheart best with a bit of couthy language chucked in for good measure? For all his political skills, Mr Cameron knows fine well he would be on a loser and that is why it will never happen.[60]

Nonetheless, Cameron did receive mild praise once the result was secured. Predictions of him becoming the 'PM who lost the Union' proved unfounded, and some commentators were quick to stress a personal victory for Cameron over Alex Salmond, particularly in light of the latter's resignation: 'There had once been talk of how canny Alex outfoxed posh Dave. Yet come cold day, it was the young Etonian's gamble that had succeeded. Salmond hooked. Salmond smoked. Ten hours later he was gone'.[61]

Of course, Cameron also received a degree of criticism for his role in the referendum. The most obvious example of this actually came after the outcome had been established, however, with the aforementioned instance where Cameron had revealed the Queen's reaction to the result. It would be front page news in some outlets, with the *Mail* highlighting that Cameron was 'to apologise to the Queen after boasting she had "purred down the line" when he called to tell her Scotland had voted No'.[62] Many seemed genuinely shocked at Cameron's indiscretion, with John MacLeod arguing:

> It is hard to know where to start with the Prime Minister's appalling conduct in New York on Tuesday, as he blithely discussed the Queen's averred pleasure at the outcome of Scotland's referendum with former New York mayor Michael Bloomberg.

MacLeod answered this by highlighting both Cameron's 'dreadful breach of the confidence that should be kept between Her Majesty and her First Lord of the Treasury' and the 'flippant, familiar language [...] in which Mr Cameron discussed his sovereign'.[63]

The letters pages also featured criticism of the Prime Minister, though this tended to focus on his lack of foresight in allowing the referendum in the first place. As one submission to the *Telegraph* argued: 'How dare David Cameron agree to allow Scotland a sole voice on its future? This was a matter for the whole of the United Kingdom, not just Scotland. If Scotland votes Yes he should resign immediately'.[64] Another drew attention to the potential predicament which Scotland could find itself should a pro-independence majority emerge, questioning the Prime Minister's overall commitment to the cause: 'Mr Cameron has left our fellow citizens in Scotland to fight a rearguard battle against the pied piper of West Lothian, leading Scotland into Nowhere Land'.[65]

Cameron may have been deliberately kept from being central to the No campaign's overall publicity machine, but there were nonetheless occasions where he briefly held the media spotlight. Both instances concerned speeches given by the Prime Minister, with particular attention devoted to the supposed emotional content of his address on each occasion. During a period in the campaigning where, as Peter Geoghegan recalls, 'it seemed that every utterance was either "emotional" or passionate"', the framing of Cameron's speeches in Edinburgh and Aberdeen proved no exception.[66] The *Times* described 'an emotional and humble appearance in front of finance workers in Edinburgh', while the *Telegraph* highlighted how 'an emotional

Mr Cameron acknowledged his party's unpopularity in Scotland, but warned that the result of next week's vote will affect the country for a century'.[67] Describing the event as 'get-real, search-your-soul stuff in front of an audience of actuaries', Quentin Letts saw the style of the speech as indicative of Cameron's unique political ability:

> He just sat there on his own on a bar-stool, rather like the late Dave Allen, and chatted extempore with throaty affection. I'm not sure anyone else in British politics could have even attempted it, let alone pulled it off with such elan.[68]

Though the wording of Cameron's speech was quoted at length, what is notable about the coverage is that the focal point of the reporting centred on Cameron's supposed emotionality in delivering these remarks. Indeed, if the content of his speech was the main part of the story, it had (with some minor alterations) already been available on the day it was publicly voiced, with Cameron granted a guest column in the 10 September edition of the *Mail*: 'Across England, Northern Ireland and Wales, our fear over what we stand to lose is matched only by our passion for what can be achieved if we stay together'.[69] An expression which most certainly did not make this published version of his speech was the use of 'effing', a linguistic device further leapt upon by the press as evidence of how deeply affected Cameron was by the issue of independence. This utterance gained a fair degree of coverage from the press, with the *Sun* beginning one report, 'David Cameron yesterday pleaded with Scots not to give the Tories an "effing" kicking as he urged Scotland to vote No', while the *Mail* cited a different version of the term's application: 'An emotional David Cameron yesterday pleaded with Scots not to use next week's referendum as a protest vote to punish the "effing Tories"'.[70] Much of the commentary on this particular outburst was rather tongue-in-cheek, though some were able to find some greater meaning in the use of the term. As Ann Treneman noted, 'It was the first time he has said "effing" on television. But then these are effing desperate times'.[71] Iain MacWhirter commented how the exchange had prompted 'a rather abstruse semantic debate [...] over whether "effing" is the same as the f-word', before noting that many Scots probably didn't 'appreciate him using language he wouldn't have used in the House of Commons'.[72] A more humorous take was offered by Quentin Letts, who provided the following sketch: 'Had the Prime Minister just said "effing"? He most certainly had. Perhaps he thought it was mandatory up here'.[73] The concept that Cameron was sincere in his professed love of Scotland within the United Kingdom was thus emphasised in the press coverage both through reference to the format of the event (not public, but more relaxed) and through his utilisation of language hitherto unused in official political discourse.

Cameron's emotional delivery further cemented the concept of the Prime Minister's concerns over the future of the United Kingdom, this being illustrated by several references to the fact that Cameron may have actually started crying during the speech. Reporting how Cameron had 'sought to match Gordon Brown in emotion', a *Herald* article would further emphasise that, 'The Tory leader appeared close to tears at one stage as he campaigned in Edinburgh'.[74] A similar evaluation appeared in a James Chapman piece for the *Mail*:

> Adding that people in the rest of the UK are "holding our breath" for the referendum result, he appeared close to tears as he reiterated his passionate appeal in yesterday's Scottish Daily Mail for the preservation of the 307-year-old Union.[75]

Notable in the coverage, both in terms of the number of sources involved but also in relation to the style of reporting, is the observation that much of the language in describing Cameron's supposed show of emotion was guarded and non-committal. All would state that he was 'close to tears', but none went as far as confirming that he had actually shed them. Indeed, there is some evidence that this aspect of the story was pure embellishment from certain contributors. For example, Quentin Letts would describe how Cameron's 'gaze shimmered like a country road's Tarmac on some steamy day', later making reference perhaps to where the idea of the near-tears originated, gently drawing attention to the theatrical nature of it all: 'And colleagues in the front row swore they saw a glint of tears in the Prime Minister's headlights. Pure Branagh!'[76] Writing in the *Times*, Ann Treneman also commented on the supposed tears and the degree to which they could be interpreted as genuine: '"I would be heartbroken if this family of nations was to tear apart", Dave said, his eyes moistening. Tears! And, worse, English tears. It looked sincere but, also, rather suspicious'.[77] That Cameron's alleged tears were at least partially fabricated by elements of the media, something of an agreed collective framing of a story that would otherwise have been made relevant only for the Prime Minister's use of 'effing', is given some credence by the following extract from Alan Cochrane's referendum diaries: 'The bad lads like me and a few others in the front rows agreed we could see a tear in his eye and so that's what appeared in the papers the next day! Disgraceful behaviour'.[78]

A similar pattern would be repeated a few days later, in the coverage of Cameron's final official speech before the vote. Attention once again focused primarily on the tone of the speech's delivery, rather than what the Prime Minister had said. 'David Cameron has made an impassioned plea to Scots to reject independence', reported a front page article in the *Herald*, with a piece in the *Scotsman* asserting that Cameron had 'made his most emotional plea for saving the UK', in what it described as 'an unashamedly patriotic speech'.[79] That the Prime Minister had been 'close to tears' was once again remarked upon, this time by the *Sun*, while the *Mail* reported that 'the Prime Minister's voice cracked repeatedly as he begged voters: "Please, please...don't turn your backs on the best family of nations in the world"'.[80] Quentin Letts discussed Cameron's 'thespy, creaky-voiced plea', going on to say of the Prime Minister: 'He lifted his eyes and it was like looking into the gaze of a spaniel that knows you have one last piece of sausage on your plate'.[81]

Taken together with observations concerning the manner in which the press framed the interventions of the Queen, it is obvious that the public remarks of both the Head of State and the Prime Minister, though largely stage-managed, nonetheless generated endless reporting and comment (usually in terms which were arguably beneficial to the pro-Unionist position). Also of note is the fact that the interventions of both David Cameron and the Queen were, on the whole, based largely upon sentimental or emotional foundations. While the No campaign often stressed the 'realities', 'hard facts' or 'rationality' of many of the key arguments against independence – with the debate being frequently characterised as being one of head over heart – it is revealing that two of the major interventions from the Unionist side in the final days of the referendum debate were almost entirely reliant on some mixture of sentiment, emotionalism or nostalgia for much of their impact.

Notes

1 JK Rowling, "JK Rowling and the risky business of separation", *Record*, 4.9.14, p. 7.
2 Kevan Christie, "Murray is hit by 'disgusting' online abuse after backing Yes campaign", *Scotsman*, 19.9.14, p. 6; David Pilditch, "Murray's regret over backing for Yes", *Express*, 24.9.14, p. 5.
3 David Clegg, "Archie raises the Woof!", *Record*, 28.8.14, p. 1.

4 Lindsay McIntosh, "Brown and Darling reunite to work better together", *Times*, 28.8.14, p. 7.
5 Magnus Gardham, "Pundit Macpherson scores for No", *Herald*, 28.8.14, p. 1.
6 Kevin Schofield, "Chindependence", *Sun*, 7.8.14, p. 6.
7 Peter Dominiczak & Georgia Graham, "Jagger joins star chorus urging Scots to vote 'No'", *Telegraph*, 8.8.14, p. 5.
8 Tom Holland, "How we drew up our love letter to Scotland", *Telegraph*, 8.8.14, p. 16.
9 Editorial, "UK wakes up to threat", *Express*, 8.8.14, p. 12.
10 Bill Leckie, "651 days on...Eck still dodges issue", *Sun*, 7.8.14, p. 11.
11 Editorial, "Strictly ludicrous", *Record*, 8.8.14, p. 6.
12 Douglas Gray, "Chance for real democracy", *Mail*, 13.8.14, p. 52; Angelica DaCosta, "Make Anne the princess of Scotland", *Sun*, 12.8.14, p. 37.
13 James Kellman, "Make Anne the princess of Scotland", *Sun*, 12.8.14, p. 37.
14 James Chapman & Rebecca English, "Queen's plea on Scots poll", *Mail*, 15.9.14, p. 1; There would also be slight variations of the Queen's remarks: Jack Doyle, "MPs applaud call by 'Queen Astute'", *Mail*, 16.9.14, p. 7; Emily Ashton, "Queen: Think Scots", *Sun*, 15.9.14, p. 1.
15 Peter Hennessy, *The Kingdom to Come: Thoughts on the Union Before and After the Referendum* (London: Haus Curiosities, 2015), p. 14.
16 James Chapman & Rebecca English, "I hope everybody thinks very carefully about the referendum", *Mail*, 15.9.14, p. 8.
17 Simon Johnson et al., "Queen breaks her silence over Scottish independence", *Telegraph*, 15.9.14, p. 1.
18 Gordon Rayner, "Queen's aside was a carefully played defence of the Union", *Telegraph*, 15.9.14, p. 5.
19 Torcuil Crichton, "I hope everybody thinks about the future this week carefully", *Record*, 15.9.14, p. 6.
20 Lindsay McIntosh, "Queen asks Scots to 'think very carefully'", *Times*, 15.9.14, p. 1.
21 Simon Johnson et al., "Queen breaks her silence"; Chapman & English, "I hope everybody thinks".
22 Chapman & English, "Queen's plea".
23 Doyle, "MPs applaud call".
24 Editorial, "Wise words", *Sun*, 15.9.14, p. 12.
25 Magnus Gardham et al., "Queen in referendum plea", *Herald*, 15.9.14, p. 1.
26 Rayner, "Queen's 'aside'".
27 Jason Beattie, "Monarch in talk with PM after poll puts Indy campaign in lead", *Record*, 8.9.14, p. 9.
28 Gordon Rayner et al., "Cameron urged to ask Queen to speak out", *Telegraph*, 9.9.14, p. 4.
29 Editorial, "Her majesty embodies the Unionist cause", *Telegraph*, 9.9.14, p. 21.
30 Greg Christison, "The Queen terrified by threat to her kingdom", *Express*, 8.9.14, p. 5; Beattie, "Monarch in talks".
31 Hamish Macdonell, "'Yes' voters don't want the Queen", *Times*, 8.9.14, p. 7; Peter McKay, "Oh, to be a fly on the wall at Balmoral", *Mail*, 8.9.14, p. 17.
32 Robert Hardman, "Queen saw this coming when Blair began his meddling", *Mail*, 9.9.14, p. 11.
33 Allison Pearson, "The Queen loves Scotland. Who would wrench it from her?", *Telegraph*, 11.9.14, p. 21.

34 Hardman, "Queen saw this coming"; Peter Oborne, "Great Britain is facing its greatest constitutional crisis in 300 years", *Telegraph*, 11.9.14, p. 22.

35 Michael Cole, "Why a victory for Salmond may see Queen step down", *Express*, 12.9.14, p. 12.

36 Chris Musson, "Purr Majesty", *Sun*, 24.9.14, p. 1.

37 Kerry Gill, "Cameron: Queen 'purred' at No vote news", *Express*, 24.9.14, p. 4; Jason Groves et al., "Forgive me, your majesty, grovels the PM after his gaffe on referendum", *Mail*, 25.9.14, p. 5.

38 John MacLeod, "Why one will definitely NOT be amused by the PM", *Mail*, 25.9.14, p. 17.

39 Cole, "Why a victory"; Sam Coates, Lindsay McIntosh & Valentine Low, "Don't drag me into this debate, says the Queen", *Times*, 10.9.14, p. 1.

40 Tom Peterkin, "Queen 'will not attempt to influence referendum", *Scotsman*, 10.9.14, p. 7; See also: Peter McKay, "Is Salmond planning to ditch the Queen?", *Mail*, 15.9.14, p. 17; Paul Gilbride, "HM 'happy to be Queen of Scots'", *Express*, 10.9.14, p. 5; Laura Elston, "Queen hails UK's 'robust democratic tradition' after vote", *Herald*, 20.9.14, p. 7.

41 Gardham et al., "Queen in referendum plea".

42 Rayner, "Queen's 'aside'".

43 Hardman, "Queen saw this coming".

44 McKay, "Oh, to be".

45 Chapman & English, "I hope everybody thinks".

46 Editorial, "Her majesty embodies".

47 Oborne, "Great Britain is facing".

48 Rayner, "Queen's 'aside'".

49 Stephen Glover, "Republicans will howl, but if the Queen doesn't speak out, she may have no United Kingdom to reign over", *Mail*, 12.9.14, p. 14.

50 Lindsay McIntosh, "Boris: No need to give Scots more power", *Times*, 11.8.14, p. 9.

51 Boris Johnson, "Scottish independence: decapitate Britain and we kill off the greatest political union ever", *Telegraph*, 8.9.14, p. 21.

52 Alex Massie, "Tories need to prove that they're people too", *Times*, 1.10.14, p. 23.

53 See: Gareth Rose, "Guess who's better at spot kicks for charity shoot-out", *Mail*, 4.9.14, p. 13.

54 Simon Johnson, "Cameron salutes Davidson's pledge of future unity", *Telegraph*, 29.9.14, p. 1.

55 Torcuil Crichton, "Ruth takes it to the max", *Record*, 29.9.14, p. 6.

56 Mike Settle, "Cameron will be damned if he does or does not", *Herald*, 27.8.14, p. 7.

57 Andrew Nicoll, "A muddle for Cam & cuddle for Salm", *Sun*, 11.9.14, p. 8.

58 Andrew Pierce, "Moment Red Ed's hopes of being PM fell apart", *Mail*, 20.9.14, p. 9.

59 Andrew Nicoll & Chris Musson, "Cam and have a go", *Sun*, 27.8.14, p. 1.

60 Editorial, "Cam too canny to take on Eck", *Sun*, 27.8.14, p. 6.

61 Quentin Letts, "One deft flick of the unconvinced voter's knife and the King of Fish lies gutted", *Mail*, 20.9.14, p. 2.

62 Jason Groves & Rebecca English, "Cameron's apology to Queen over No vote gaffe", *Mail*, 24.9.14, p. 1.

63 MacLeod, "Why one will".

64 Bret Johnson, "David Cameron must resign immediately if Scotland chooses to vote in favour of separation", *Telegraph*, 9.9.14, p. 21.

65 Prof SF Bush, *Ibid.*

66 Peter Geoghegan, *The People's Referendum: Why Scotland Will Never Be The Same Again* (Edinburgh: Luath Press, 2015), p. 120.

67 Lindsay McIntosh et al., "Don't break Union just to give Tories a kicking, pleads tearful Cameron", *Times*, 11.9.14, p. 6; Peter Dominiczak & Christopher Hope, "Don't vote Yes to give 'effing' Tories a kick, says Cameron", *Telegraph*, 11.9.14, p. 4.

68 Quentin Letts, "No razzmatazz, no script – this was a raw, emotional Dave", *Mail*, 11.9.14, p. 7.

69 David Cameron, "We must write the next chapter in our history together", *Mail*, 10.9.14, p. 5.

70 Andrew Nicoll, "Efferendum", *Sun*, 11.9.14, p. 4; James Chapman, "Cameron: It's not about the effing Tories", *Mail*, 11.9.14, p. 6.

71 Ann Treneman, "Team Westminster try the broken-heart ploy (and Dave swears by it)", *Times*, 11.9.14, p. 7.

72 MacWhirter, "The 'effing referendum'".

73 Letts, "No razzmatazz".

74 Kate Devlin, "Cameron: Don't vote Yes to kick the 'effing Tories'", *Herald*, 11.9.14, p. 5.

75 Chapman, "Cameron: It's not about".

76 Letts, "No razzmatazz".

77 Treneman, "Team Westminster".

78 Alan Cochrane, *Alex Salmond: My Part in His Downfall* (London: Biteback Publishing, 2014), pp. 306–307.

79 Kate Devlin & Michael Settle, "Heartbroken if you leave", *Herald*, 16.9.14, p. 1; Tom Peterkin, "Don't break our hearts, PM pleads with Scottish voters", *Scotsman*, 16.9.14, p. 4.

80 Chris Musson & Andrew Nicoll, "Sob Tory", *Sun*, 16.9.14, p. 4; James Chapman, "I won't be here forever...please don't split this UK family apart", *Mail*, 16.9.14, p. 6.

81 Quentin Letts, "Sad Dave, sugary as a foreman's cuppa", *Mail*, 16.9.14, p. 6.

6   Beast mode

Darling, Brown and the Labour Party

The general unpopularity of the Conservatives in Scotland ensured that public interventions from even the Prime Minister were both rare and heavily mediated. With the deciding votes in the referendum thought likely to depend on Labour voters, combined with the party's high levels of traditional support in the former industrial heartlands, it therefore fell to the Labour Party to spearhead the campaign to retain Scotland's place in the Union.

The Labour Vanguard

With Alistair Darling as the public face of Better Together from the earliest days of the official campaign, Labour was central to arguing the case for the Union throughout the referendum process. It was only in September, however, that a concerted effort on the part of the UK Labour Party shifted into higher gear, with a series of poll results provoking a panicked response from London politicians who had largely remained distant to that point. Though belated in their interventions, that Labour became the dominant voice for Better Together was entirely predictable, given the party's long-standing popularity in Scotland. As a *Times* editorial highlighted, 'In the last weeks of the campaign, it falls upon Labour to make a better case for Better Together'.[1] While accepted with a subtle begrudging tone in some right-of-centre titles, others were actively enthusiastic about the important position Labour now found itself occupying. 'In the end the referendum debate has come down to the Labour Party. It was always going to. The party that made modern Scotland is the one that has to save it', wrote John McTernan, further advocating for the more visible inclusion of those who could help propagate

DOI: 10.4324/9781003138259-6

the Labour position to those traditionally favourable to the party's message:

> it's all the preachers of old time religion – from John Prescott and Dennis Skinner to Owen Jones – who need to be up here, on street corners, in schemes, in tenants' halls across the country. A core vote strategy needs core vote voices and Labour should use the best.[2]

Ultimately, what Scotland received was a rushed and hastily arranged collective Labour onslaught, triggered by the fact that the referendum was viewed as being 'on a knife edge', with 'traditional Labour voters expected to decide the result'.[3] Indeed, some were eager to point out that the only reason such an intervention was necessary was as a result of Labour's poor management of the No campaign to that point. Focusing on the efforts of Better Together, a *Mail* editorial would opine:

> What is unforgivable is that almost no serious planning seems to have gone into this amateurish display while much of the talking has been left to discredited, uninspiring Labour politicians, many of whom can't stand the sight of each other.[4]

That the campaign was struggling due to the failures of Labour-led decisions was also raised much earlier in the coverage, with a submission to the *Scotsman* arguing that the referendum was 'only taking place because of the failures of our political leaders, in particular the Scottish Labour party'.[5] Regardless of political leaning, the mass gathering of Labour politicians in Glasgow (and selected other local events), for example, nonetheless attracted several pages of news and comment. Notable, however, is that some of this coverage was actually quite critical in tone or content. As Kate Devlin would write, with a certain humorous cynicism: 'William loved Scotland, Harriet loved Scotland and MPs from both sides of the House were blowing kisses northwards towards those lovely people beyond Hadrian's Wall. PMQs had turned into one giant love letter to Caledonia'.[6] Coverage in the *Sun* drew attention to the fact that Westminster-based politicians – of various political colours – were revealing a level of concern (or desperation) by acting out such a publicity-friendly jaunt north of the border, with Chris Musson reporting how the party leaders had 'summoned English reinforcements amid panic at a stuttering performance'.[7]

Not all coverage of Labour framed the party's more vocal defenders of the Union in such disorganised or opportunistic terms, with several Labour big-hitters receiving generally positive coverage, even in those outlets historically inclined to push a pro-Conservative position. For example, as Alan Roden remarked of Jim Murphy's return to his street-campaign: 'He strutted towards the crowd like a champion boxer, flanked by a furry mascot and sending his adoring fans wild'.[8] The *Express* would continue this particular trend, which might be thought of as a political ceasefire on the part of the press, at least in relation to certain members of the party. As Kerry Gill discussed: 'one thing is sure. Brown, Darling and Lamont will be remembered for doing their level best to save the Union, while innumerable other members of their party will be remembered, if at all, for doing next to nothing'.[9] Even Alan Cochrane of the *Telegraph* celebrated the arrival of some of Labour's bigger beasts to argue the case for the Union: 'again, it is Labour people who must be in the vanguard of this. It is, thus, immensely heartening that Gordon Brown, John Reid and, even if he's not Labour, Charlie Kennedy are now rushing to the "No Thanks" banner'.[10]

This observation – whereby anti-Labour titles and contributors would, temporarily in the weeks before the referendum, adapt the tone of their coverage to be at best celebratory and at worst less critical of their former Labour targets – reached its zenith with Alistair Darling and Gordon Brown, though the framing of Ed Miliband provides reason to adapt this conclusion. Leader of the Labour Party in 2014, Miliband did not become the focus of press attention, in relation to the independence debate, to the extent which one might have assumed. Though the same issues which impacted upon Cameron's limited visibility (regarding the optics of an English politician being seen to dictate on a Scottish issue) also applied, to an extent, to the Labour leader, the coverage further reveals that discourse surrounding Miliband, with the exception of the Labour-supporting *Record*, tended to be rather critical both of his role in the debate and of him personally.

Though speculative, one assumption can at least be made concerning the fact that Miliband was portrayed in the manner described: that the potential for him to be Prime Minister after the following year's general election meant that several right-leaning newspapers tailored their coverage of the referendum to also, though rarely explicitly, dissuade those who may have considered voting for Miliband and his party. The leader of the Labour Party may have been expected to generate a similar level of positive framing from the press as that afforded the likes of backbench MPs or former grandees of the party; however, since polls indicated that Miliband had a realistic chance of becoming Prime Minister in 2015, it was against their larger editorial agenda to publicise him in a way which could have lasting benefits for his standing with the electorate. Neither Gordon Brown nor Alistair Darling was conceived as being a genuine political threat, and therefore Conservative-supporting titles championing or lionising these politicians – even though they were Labour – came with less long-term risk than endorsing or positively framing Ed Miliband, at least in relation to the upcoming general election.

On balance, most criticism of Miliband was fairly mild, at least in the period before the result of the referendum was known. As the *Sun* reported: 'Ed Miliband urged Scots to snub independence as he bragged he will be PM – before Alex Salmond branded him clueless'.[11] Coverage from early September opined that Miliband appeared to be ignoring the referendum debate in favour of the approaching general election, by openly criticising the Conservatives even as a temporary alliance was apparently in place between the parties: 'Ed Miliband caused a major rift in the campaign to prevent the break-up of Britain yesterday by defying appeals from Alistair Darling to stop attacking Ruth Davidson, the Scottish Tory leader'.[12] The *Sun* would further comment on this theme, of whether Miliband was sufficiently focused on the issue at hand, in an editorial: 'It was hard to figure out exactly what Ed Miliband was campaigning for yesterday. To help save the United Kingdom at this month's referendum, or an election victory next May'.[13] The *Times* struck a less accusatory tone, highlighting how a Miliband speech had at least demonstrated 'rather belatedly, that he realises what is at stake', while repeating the criticism that he should have been more involved earlier in the campaign.[14]

Almost immediately following the confirmation of the result, however, any small pretence of an understanding between the centre-right press and Labour all but fell apart. With the correct result secured (in the opinion of the explicitly Unionist titles), the political focus now shifted to the 2015 general election, and so the short-lived political ceasefire between Labour and the right-leaning titles came to an abrupt end with the majority for No. As Andrew Pierce noted of Miliband, in a piece published on 20 September: 'What he neglected to admit, of course, was that his own role in the No campaign had been shambolic from start to finish'.[15] On the issue of new powers being devolved to Scotland, and the degree to which the rushed proposals could impact on Labour's election hopes, Jenni Russell would write:

> The promise of more power for Scotland along with continued high subsidies has left people wondering if they are being taken for a ride [...] Ed Miliband's and Ed Balls' prevarications on the subject have left them looking blind to English fears.[16]

That the leader of the Labour Party should have been ignored or marginalised should not be read, however, as an indication that this was the case for other members of his party. As mentioned, the wider Labour Party gained a notable degree of positive coverage during the referendum debate, even from those titles historically averse to supporting the party, with no two individuals benefitting from this arrangement more so than Alistair Darling and Gordon Brown.

The steady pair of hands: Alistair Darling

As the man chosen to lead the Better Together campaign, Alistair Darling regained a relevance and legitimacy in political life which had eluded him since 2010, when his time as Chancellor had ended. Involved in various photo-ops, endorsements and other campaign events, Darling was something of an ever-present during the debate, with his prominent position in the No campaign only undermined in the very final weeks leading to the vote. This is not to say, of course, that his leadership to that point had been flawless. One such mis-step came with his unveiling of a series of posters, featuring slogans such as 'We love our kids. We're saying No Thanks', which the *Mail* generously described as 'a series of highly emotive referendum adverts'.[17] The *Times* was less guarded in reporting this controversial unveiling, with Hamish Macdonell reporting, 'Alistair Darling provoked anger from the Yes campaign yesterday when he unveiled posters that appeared to suggest that people who loved their families should vote "no" in the referendum'.[18] Such gaffes were rare from Darling, however, with the press generally framing him as a steady pair of hands. Indeed, despite having been replaced by Gordon Brown as the No campaign's figurehead, Darling was still granted guest commentary space in the days leading to the vote. In one such piece in the *Mail*, Darling drew attention to the UK's shared achievements:

> We faced down fascism in the Second World War, standing alone for many months, we founded and built the most socially just health service in the world; and the UK had the strength to withstand the financial crash that crippled other countries.

The article would go on to beseech those supporting No to go out and actually vote, while also emphasising the crucial nature of the result: 'So please act. I'm not exaggerating when I say Thursday is probably the most important day of our democratic lives'.[19] A similarly worded piece, echoing the aforementioned poster campaign by focusing on the topic of family, appeared in the *Scotsman* on the day of the vote, thus representing one of Darling's last major contributions to the referendum process. 'Why take such a huge risk with our future, the future of our children and the future of our health service when faster, better, safer change is coming to Scotland within the UK?', challenged Darling, 'We should vote No because we don't have to be a separate nation to be a better nation'.[20]

Beyond his speeches, occasional press contributions or other campaign-related activities, Darling was the focus of concentrated newspaper attention on only a handful of instances. One of these came in the attention given to his political reunion with Gordon Brown, with their first public appearance together in four years often framed as indicative of how concerned the No campaign had become. 'Alistair Darling and Gordon Brown will call a truce in their feud today as they unite to keep Britain together', reported the front page of the *Record*, with the *Times* also featuring the reunion on page one.[21] Describing how they would 'put aside today one of the bitterest feuds in British political history when they stand shoulder to shoulder to fight against Scottish independence', Lindsay McIntosh further emphasised how the public reconciliation between the former Prime Minister and former Chancellor was 'an indication of how tough the fight for the Union has become'.[22] As the same author commented the following day, 'The men fell out politically and professionally at the end of Labour's time in office but, yesterday, they put their differences aside to fight for the United Kingdom', and general coverage of the event tended to be accompanied by images – of Brown and Darling sharing a smile, for instance – which illustrated the supposed thawing of relations between the two.[23] Few articles questioned the sincerity of the purported renewal of the men's relationship, though some were more guarded in discussing the apparent friendship. 'They were back together but would they be better together? Or even just all right together?', queried Magnus Gardham in the *Herald*, 'They affected, at least, a public display of affection'.[24] In this particular instance, however, one can surmise that it was the re-emergence of Gordon Brown – who until that point had restricted himself to lower-level Labour events – as a main player for the pro-Unionist cause which was the real focus of such coverage. Certainly, rather than marking the end of a political feud, it was with the benefit of hindsight instead an introduction and coronation of Brown to a more visible leadership role within the Better Together campaign.

Darling's most publicised (and celebrated) interventions, however, followed the two televised debates with Alex Salmond, with his performance in the first outing gaining widespread praise from myriad press outlets. Darling was not considered a natural media performer, and Better Together advisers had private reservations regarding his ability to match Salmond in the setting of a televised debate.[25] However, in what was billed as 'what could be a landmark moment in the battle for Scotland', the former Chancellor put in a far stronger appearance than expected.[26] Indeed, many commentators were apparently caught off guard by the tone and effectiveness of Darling's STV debate showing, with resulting opinion near unanimous that he had emerged victorious over a lacklustre First Minister. Darling, who had been 'expected to struggle against the charismatic Mr Salmond' in the words of Lindsay McIntosh, 'was quickly on the front foot with a statesman-like performance'.[27] Other commentary highlighted the contrast between Darling's subdued persona and his more engaged debate performance. 'For a man with a reputation as a dry-as-dust bank manager', noted a *Mail* editorial, 'Alistair Darling mounted a strikingly impressive performance in the first televised debate on the referendum'.[28] This was echoed by Magnus Linklater, who emphasised both Darling's image and the forceful nature of his debating style:

> This was not at all what we expected. Billed as a contest between a political bruiser and the nation's bank manager, it turned out in the end to be a case of one angry man: and that man, far from being Alex Salmond, was Alistair Darling.

As Linklater would conclude: 'At least we learnt one thing: Alistair Darling may be the grey man of British politics, but dull he is not'.[29]

That Darling had comfortably won the exchange was the key takeaway for many of the newspapers featured, and praise for his performance continued to build in the days following the 5 August debate. Alan Roden reiterated that, 'Mr Salmond's failure to provide a plan B for a separate currency was masterfully exposed by the former Chancellor', with the *Sun* in agreement that 'Mr Darling's big weapon and best spell of the contest was hammering home the uncertainty over currency'.[30] 'It was a hammering, pure and simple', asserted Alan Cochrane in his *Telegraph* column, 'astonishingly for some, it was the allegedly "boring" former chancellor who raised the temperature brilliantly with a scintillating attack on Alex Salmond'.[31] Alex Massie's commentary would also emphasise the scale of Darling's victory by stating that 'Rarely has Mr Salmond been beaten up so badly live on television', though his analysis bordered on the surreal the following day, where he compared Darling to Conan the Barbarian:

> As in warfare, so in politics and, if it remains odd to think of Alistair Darling inhabiting a role made famous by Arnold

Schwarzenegger, it remains the case that he crushed Alex Salmond in Tuesday night's referendum debate in Glasgow.[32]

Of course, even in those sources actively supporting a No vote, the coverage of the Better Together leader was not uniformly positive. Particularly following the second televised debate (where Salmond was generally adjudged to have emerged the victor), Darling came in for varying degrees of criticism. Critical submissions to the letters pages occasionally stressed the fact that Darling was seen as a career politician, such as in an example from the *Express* which derided Darling as 'a yesterday's man with anglocentric views, who, like so many others depends on a No vote to further their political futures in Westminster'.[33] Others pointed to the fact that the right-leaning press had been all too eager to praise Darling, while seemingly forgetting that their own past coverage had tended towards the negative when discussing the former Chancellor: 'The Tory press used to crucify Alistair Darling when he was Labour Chancellor. Now that he has become a true blue English Tory [...] he is a pin up. The hypocrisy makes you sick'.[34]

Questions were also raised regarding Darling's suitability for such a leadership role, an issue which became more pressing in the aftermath of the second televised debate. The *Sun* would be especially critical of Darling in this regard, with an editorial piece speculating, 'Many of the don't knows watching at home and waiting to be convinced will have found [Salmond's] passion hard to resist and the Better Together chief's dithering doom-mongering just as hard to admire'.[35] In the same edition, Bill Leckie would further remark: 'a man with the First Minister's savvy should never have been playing catch-up with Darling in the first place'.[36] Further contributions emphasised that Darling's personality, once cited as a strength, had now become a liability: 'Alistair Darling lost Monday's independence debate so thoroughly because he is unable to present himself as a person of the people'.[37] A Graham Grant piece for the *Mail*, published after the referendum and reflecting on the performances of various politicians, highlighted several of these aforementioned issues. Highlighting that 'Mr Darling's dour bank manager persona was identified as Better Together's greatest weakness', Grant would further describe how Darling had lost 'some of his sure-footedness as Mr Brown took centre-stage [...] In this context, Mr Darling is surely one of the "losers" – though his personal dedication to the cause can never be in doubt'.[38]

Judging by the press coverage from the period, Alistair Darling – despite being the official leader of the Better Together campaign – was only occasionally the main focal point of press interest. A reliable if uncharismatic politician, Darling was ultimately replaced by Gordon Brown in the final weeks leading to the vote, with the former Prime Minister generating a degree of coverage which far surpassed virtually anything afforded his former cabinet colleague in the months prior.

The biggest beast: Gordon Brown

With opinion polls showing a significant movement towards Yes as the campaign entered the crucial early weeks of September, it was widely believed that the No campaign needed a boost to ensure their desired result. Indeed, the apparent lack of engagement from the official No campaign had been remarked upon for several weeks already, as seen in the following letter to the *Mail*: 'If, God forbid, we get independence, the Better Together campaign will be partly responsible for not being visible and pro-active enough'.[39] This apparent collective desire to both shore up the Unionist vote and persuade those still undecided would be partially addressed by the aforementioned interventions of the Queen and David Cameron, though again it should be stressed that in both cases the words used, the tone of their utterances and the type of access granted to the media and the public were all carefully choreographed. Evidently, the Better Together campaign required a known political personality – ideally Scottish – who could deliver the No campaign's message to the masses, especially those sections of the electorate who had traditionally voted Labour. Step forward Gordon Brown, who was swiftly established as the official voice of the campaign, and in doing so went on to receive a level of positive coverage which had eluded him for several years. '[The] shrinkage in support was overwhelmingly among very "culturally Labour" people meaning Better Together needed a trusted Labour figure to communicate their counterargument', noted Joe Pike, who further revealed, 'At one meeting, the shared conclusion was: "There aren't many problems to which the solution is 'Send for Gordon Brown!' But this most definitely is one"'.[40]

The terms of Brown's leadership were clearly laid out in the press, few of whom shied away from interpreting his late introduction to the frontline of the campaign as evidence of the genuine concern over the possibility of Scotland becoming independent. 'Gordon Brown was parachuted in to save the Union last night', reported the *Times*, adding that the 'eleventh-hour decision to seek Mr Brown's help represents a significant U-turn by the No campaign'.[41] The *Record* also stressed the apparent jeopardy of the United Kingdom, with one editorial asserting how the newspaper had already 'warned starkly that the No campaign had just 10 days left to save the Union', before advocating for Gordon Brown to be the leading voice of such a defence.[42] As was the case with other traditionally Conservative contributors and their temporarily revised treatment of Labour politicians and campaigners, Brown's new integral role in the defence of the Union ensured that he received a notable degree of positive coverage from sources histori- cally predisposed to critiquing the former Prime Minister both pro- fessionally and personally. 'And yet, as Britain teeters on the verge of break-up, it falls to the former prime minister to save his native Scotland from itself to preserve Britain's 300-year-old Union. Gordon the Great Redeemer is the most curious example of political casting in recent memory', wrote Mary Riddell in the *Telegraph*, in a hearty endorsement of Brown's perhaps unique suitability for such an im- portant role. 'Not since Caligula supposedly appointed his horse as a consul has the political elite arrived at an odder choice [...] Mr Brown slips smoothly into the role of saviour', insisted Riddell, 'The man who saved the world [...] after the financial crash may be the only statesman with the experience and heft to deal with the greatest crisis that the UK has faced since the near-collapse of the global economy'.[43]

Among the crucial roles adopted by Gordon Brown in this later campaign push was that of the trusted messenger; someone with the appropriate political recognition and legitimacy to propagate the supposedly revised and improved offer of more powers to Scotland in the event of a No vote. With the benefit of hindsight, the cover- age of Brown in this regard – which would be largely uncritical of his claims, nor cynical about either his ability to deliver them or indeed his right to even offer them – may be seen as a crucial aspect of the later campaign. Although the new offer of increased devolved pow- ers featured very little which was not already on the table, and had already been endorsed by the three main UK party leaders, it fell to Gordon Brown to act as the trusted guarantor of looming political change should Scotland decide to remain part of the United King- dom. A notable peak of such coverage came on 9–10 September, where Brown's alleged brokering of a new-deal regarding greatly enhanced powers for the Scottish Parliament gained widespread exposure. Many of the headlines during this period took the former Prime Minister entirely at his word, framing the promises of a backbench MP in a remarkably uncritical manner. 'He effectively handed a loaded gun to the Tories and Lib Dems, offering them the choice of either backing the plan or blowing their one chance to save the Union', celebrated the *Record*, going on to place the newspaper itself at the root cause of Brown's intervention: 'Brown made the move hours after the Record demanded that the pro-union parties spell out a coherent alternative for Scotland's future'.[44] Notably, the period in question revealed a further trend of typically centre-right titles affording explicitly positive coverage to an individual formerly criticised, ridiculed or otherwise derided. For example, as the *Telegraph* would report on page one: 'The former Prime Minister unveiled a fast-track timetable for "nothing less than a modern form of Scottish Home Rule"'.[45] The theme of Brown as all but guaranteeing a version of Home Rule was also trumpeted unquestionably by the *Mail*, as in the following headline: '*Home Rule Bill' starts the day after a No vote.*[46] Indeed, even the *Express* readily endorsed Brown's late intervention. 'Former Prime Minister Gordon Brown has emerged as a late, but very welcome, champion of Scotland remaining in the United Kingdom', gushed one such editorial, 'His pledge of further powers for Holyrood, back by the other Unionist parties, were widely welcomed'.[47]

The culmination of this process came with the 16 September publication of the *Record's* front page heralding *THE VOW*, an apparent cross-party guarantee of Scotland being granted new powers in the event of a No vote. Although Brown was not one of the signatories to this joint declaration from Cameron, Clegg and Miliband, he was nonetheless instrumental both in its formulation and in its presentation through the media. As Joe Pike related of the days leading to the publication of this memorable headline:

> That afternoon, *Daily Record* editor Murray Foote texted Bruce Waddell, a predecessor at the paper, who was now handling media relations for Gordon Brown: "Would Gordon be able to get the three party leaders to sign an agreed *Daily Record* pledge for more devolved powers [...]? We could then present that as a front-page document".[48]

Indeed, the dissemination and legitimisation of this document – which did little more than repeat previously offered terms – was established by the *Record* in the days preceding the publication of the front page in question. 'Gordon Brown has secured a Commons debate next month on increasing powers to the Scottish Parliament', reported an article from 15 September, 'All three party leaders have signed up to the plan to get an enhanced devolution package on the statute books by Burns night next year – January 25 – in the event of a No vote in the referendum'.[49] Evidently, though Brown's name was not on the document, the fingerprints of his influence most certainly were, a point deliberately stressed by the *Record*, which during this period would position

Brown as having the ability to hold the UK government to some kind of account (apparently ignoring the fact that the former Prime Minister was a backbench MP *and* in the party of Opposition).

Brown's interventions in this period were not, of course, without their detractors. Commentators favouring a Yes vote were particularly suspicious of both Brown and the true intentions of the wider Unionist campaign regarding the devolution of further powers.

> I want to apologise to the people of Wales and Northern Ireland – not to mention the good folk of England. Without consulting you, and with absolutely no mandate, the leaders of the three main pro-Union parties have decided to tear up the existing British constitution and invent a new one on the back of the proverbial fag packet,

lamented George Kerevan, who would go on to warn, with some degree of foresight:

> I have no doubt that the pro-Union parties will attempt to keep to their "iron timetable" on giving more powers to Holyrood. If they don't, Labour will pay a terrible price in lost Scottish seats in next year's General Election.[50]

Other outlets highlighted that the offer of further powers played somewhat fast and loose with the rules regards electioneering, with the *Sun* describing a hypothetical-but-remarkably-similar case as 'a sneaky, behind-the-scenes deal to get round the ban on new legislation being announced during the official polling period', going on to rhetorically assert, 'Surely no one would try anything like that on, so close to the referendum'. As the editorial would continue: 'Step forward Gordon Brown as the played saviour of the Union by announcing beefed-up devolution for Scotland if independence is rejected. He is not a member of the UK government so he can get away with it'.[51]

The issue of further powers reverberated after the result was known, and Brown continued to be recognised as integral to this ongoing process. Tellingly, however, by the 20 September editions of most newspapers (generally the first to definitively report on both the referendum result and the resignation of Alex Salmond), the narrative had already shifted to stressing the difficulties with realising promises made only days before. The main point of contention was the altered position of the Westminster parties, who now insisted the transfer of further devolved powers should be considered alongside similar proposals for other nations and regions of the UK. As the *Record*'s Torcuil Crichton reported of Brown: 'The Kirkcaldy MP – who is credited with winning the vote for the No campaign – believes the real test will be to ensure that David Cameron, Ed Miliband and Nick Clegg keep their vow to Scots'.[52] Andrew Nicoll further emphasised Brown's unconvincing role in guaranteeing a powers package, which now seemed increasingly unlikely to materialise in the form promised: 'The fact is that Brown's intervention, repeating promises already made long before by all three parties, seems to have won the referendum for the No campaign'.[53] Such a critique echoed the thoughts of Joyce McMillan, who was also evidently sceptical regarding the offer of powers and the prospects for their implementation: 'my own view is that Scottish civil society would be well advised to take a long, hard look, before welcoming top-down plans thrown together by David Cameron and Gordon Brown at such insultingly short notice'.[54] By early October, it was readily apparent that the transfer of further powers would be neither as swift nor as far-reaching as appearances might have first suggested, and Brown remained central to the framing of this post-referendum issue. Scottish-only titles, such as the *Herald* and the *Record*, presented the narrative as being the Westminster party leaders who were reneging on the supposed deal, with Brown's obvious role in the original offer often being somewhat overlooked. 'Brown, whose passionate campaigning gave the No campaign vital momentum before the referendum, said Cameron could not move the goalposts on a deal voted for in good faith', reported David Clegg, before further positioning the *Record* as an important influence in the ongoing process: 'And [Brown] said he would sign the petition backed by the Daily Record calling for the vow to be honoured with no new stipulations'.[55]

Centre-right titles had, on the whole, by this point reduced their coverage of the referendum to a fraction of what it had been in the weeks immediately preceding the vote, and the issue of more powers for Scotland received limited attention in the likes of the *Mail* or the *Express* once the result was secured. Writing in the *Sun*, however, Andrew Nicoll highlighted, less than two weeks after the vote, that the offer of further powers was already looking unreliable. 'Gordon Brown repackaged [the offer of powers] in September, tied it up in tartan ribbon with an egg timer attached to the bow and called it a vow. If you didn't bother to look inside then, I'm sorry, you've got nobody to blame but yer ain sel', commented Nicoll, further criticising the fact that Brown's offer had itself fallen short of expectations: 'Although he talked of something "close to federalism" the plan Mr Brown offers is way less than even the Tories suggested'.[56] The degree to which the offer of greater devolved powers had any notable impact on voting intentions is speculative at best, but it remains the case that Gordon Brown was integral in presenting and endorsing such plans. Many of his statements and claims were published uncritically, but it is also evident that some commentators were often not prepared to take such an offer simply at face value.

One aspect of his intervention in the referendum debate which gained near universal positive coverage however was Brown's oratory on the issue of independence, with coverage of his speeches almost ubiquitous in celebrating both the content and the delivery of virtually every public declaration he gave in the weeks before 18 September. Being a traditionally Labour-leaning newspaper, the *Record* was quick to establish Brown as the main voice of the No campaign, praising the wisdom of both his appointment and his own role in stemming the apparent tide of Labour voters to the pro-independence camp. 'Since the national emergency was declared and Gordon Brown came back as PM with a Saltire over Downing Street, he has been seen as the man of the moment', noted Torcuil Crichton, whose *Record* colleague, David Clegg, went on to emphasise that Brown had 'been credited with helping turn around the fortunes of the unionists'.[57] Drawing particular attention to Brown's recent speech-making, the *Record* would – as was the case with the framing of Cameron's speeches in various titles – highlight the emotional tone and resonance of Brown's public utterances. 'The ex-PM in full flow truly is a force to be reckoned with', asserted one such editorial, 'and when he spoke about the NHS care his late daughter Jennifer Jane received it came straight from the heart'.[58]

Positive reporting of Brown's speech-making was not restricted, however, to those outlets which favoured the Labour Party. As Kerry Gill, writing a week before the vote, would wonder: 'Dare I say it? Has Gordon Brown become the man who saved the United Kingdom?'[59] A *Telegraph* opinion piece went one further, commenting that Brown's intervention may have also saved his political legacy: 'if Scotland votes No, then Gordon the Redeemer will not only have helped save the Union and his party. The prophet who went unheeded in his united land will also have secured his own redemption'.[60] Even contributors to the *Mail* would highlight the former Prime Minister's emotive performances, with Gareth Rose reporting that Gordon Brown 'invoked his daughter's death in an emotional attack on the SNP's desperate duplicity over the NHS' and had been 'almost in tears'.[61] The *Mail*'s Quentin Letts heaped additional praise on Brown's public performance, though failed to resist the urge to gently draw attention to some of the ex-Prime Minister's apparent failings: 'Gordon! Suddenly back in the stirrup, taking grip of the Better Together campaign. Uh-oh! Actually, in a very Gordonish way, making some terrible jokes about football and Nelson Mandela and smiling like Mike Yarwood, he was rather good'. Letts continued his positive assessment of Brown's speech, describing him as 'Growly, prowling the stage, grabbing the air with two big paws', also concluding that his late intervention might prove to have longer-term effects on Brown's political standing: 'This independence referendum has certainly given him a chance to recraft his reputation. This Brown, confident, roaming, was hardly recognisable from the shrivelled tomato of 2010'.[62] Such a treatment was repeated by Alan Cochrane, who endorsed the choice of Brown to lead the final stages of the No campaign. 'He may have lost the south of England, but the Great Broon is still a star turn with Scottish Labour stalwarts', opined one such column, with Cochrane going on to grudgingly accept both the limitations and unique strengths of Brown as a champion of the Unionist cause: 'The former Prime Minister may be, at times, a difficult man to work with, but he is the one politician in Scotland who can match, or even outdo, the aura and clout of Alex Salmond'.[63]

Praise of Brown's speeches, general performance and overall impact continued through to the day of the vote and beyond. Certainly, although both David Cameron and the Queen had intervened in some much-publicised fashion in the same period, by polling day it was Brown who had been placed front and centre of the No campaign. Writing on 18 September, Alan Roden would remark, 'Clearly Better Together needed a new "big beast"', going on to stress Brown's efforts in reinvigorating what was seen as a faltering campaign: 'As referendum day drew nearer, this [schedule] turned into a tsunami of town hall speeches'.[64] The emotional nature of Brown's address would be emphasised once more, with the *Scotsman* reporting that Brown had 'made an emotional plea to Scots to "hold their heads high" and act with dignity', while coverage in the *Sun* – highlighting Brown's 'impassioned last-minute plea yesterday for Scots to save the Union' – asserted it had been the former Prime Minister's 'own rousing address to hundreds of Better Together supporters that brought the house down'.[65] Describing his 17 September speech both as a 'tub-thumping, angrily passionate address' and as being 'punctuated by cheering, foot stamping and clapping, which seemed to rock the community centre in the Maryhill area of Glasgow', Lindsay McIntosh continued this general trend of framing Brown as having finally found a political relevance which had long eluded him: 'Gordon Brown rediscovered yesterday the political drive and fury that he lost as prime minister'.[66]

Evidently, to a degree arguably indicative of the panic over a pro-independence vote within elements of the Union-supporting titles, the press were happy to accept Brown as a late substitute for Alistair Darling and eager to provide the former PM's intervention with the coverage necessary to mount an effective campaign.

Such coverage continued after the result, with several contributions, some with a tone approaching relief, quick to give Brown the credit in regard to securing the pro-Union majority. Indeed, as the *Scotsman* reported, even Brown's long-time political opponents were happy to grant him due deference for his role in preserving the United Kingdom: 'Senior Conservatives in Better Together suggested the dramatic late intervention by Labour big-hitters such as Gordon Brown and John Reid had helped to save the ailing No campaign from defeat'.[67] Remarking that, 'After he was ousted from office four years ago in the midst of economic turmoil, he was a much-diminished and derided figure', Graham Grant would ultimately insist that Brown was far from a spent force: 'But his high-voltage speech in Maryhill, Glasgow, this week – a masterclass in rousing oratory – reminded friends and enemies alike of his awesome skills'.[68] Ann Treneman of the *Times* would argue, 'Without him and his marvellous ranting total-rage events, the result would have been, at the very least, much closer', while a letter to the *Herald* would express a personal appreciation of Brown's intervention: 'Watching Gordon Brown's magnificent speech last week was, for me, a release [...] His "permission" granted to us all – permission to be proud of our shared British identity – I found incredibly cathartic'.[69]

Evidently, though he had only been centre-stage in the debate for a matter of weeks, Gordon Brown found himself an important figure in British politics once again; an observation which owes much to the generally positive coverage he received from most press outlets, including those which had for several years typically framed Brown as a subject for criticism or derision. Such was Brown's short-lived impact, in fact, that there was talk of a move into the frontline of Scottish politics, despite the fact that Brown had already described his Westminster career-status as semi-retired. The prospect of Brown becoming a prominent force in Holyrood attracted coverage from several newspapers, even though few committed statements to this effect had actually been uttered. 'Gordon Brown yesterday hinted he could return to front-line politics – to take on Alex Salmond', reported the *Sun*, with the *Record* mirroring the use of rather guarded language: 'Determined Gordon Brown yesterday hinted that he might be forced to stand as an MSP to stop nationalists "peddling lies" on the NHS'.[70] The *Mail* was more forthright in its coverage of Brown's possible return, however, reporting instead that 'Gordon Brown has vowed to make a sensational political comeback if Alex Salmond persists with his "lie" about threats to Scotland's NHS'.[71] The hypothetical move to Holyrood politics ultimately did not materialise, though one can speculate that several contributors were well aware of this fact, but remained content to publicise a story which could, by extension, strengthen claims that Brown would be close at hand to force the issue of new powers with Westminster.

Nonetheless, several commentators continued to endorse such a move for Brown, seeing his introduction to Scottish politics as a necessary counterweight to the ambitions of the SNP. 'The presence of Gordon Brown at Holyrood, boosted by his remarkable performances during the referendum campaign, would surely be enough to defeat the SNP in 2016', asserted Kerry Gill, celebrating Brown's potential role in a desired change to the Scottish political landscape.[72] Describing Brown as the 'man of the moment' and as having 'fought a brilliant campaign to save the United Kingdom', an editorial in the *Express* also endorsed Brown's ambitions as an MSP: 'The Nationalists need a strong and highly experienced opponent, and Mr Brown would be the person who could fill that role'.[73] Assessing the comparative performances of various political figures in the independence debate, Graham Grant would state that the 'failure to deploy [Brown's] talents earlier in the campaign [...] now seems a strategic error', going on to mention that others saw Brown as a potential replacement for Alex Salmond: 'Re-energised and suddenly a dynamic figure once again, a range of possibilities opens up for him, including – possibly – Holyrood; some have spoken of him as a future First Minister'.[74]

Receiving positive news coverage, ringing editorial endorsements and gushing commentary, one can view these last few weeks of the referendum campaign as something of a last hurrah for Gordon Brown. Thought of as increasingly irrelevant to both the Labour Party and UK politics more generally in the years prior to the referendum, Brown was instead, in the space of a mere few weeks, returned to a place approaching relevance and respect. Given his political profile and his time in office, however, Brown inevitably also drew criticism from some quarters. In early September, for example, when Brown was emerging as the key voice of the No campaign, the centre-right press would critique his apparent ongoing attacks on the Conservative party. Mirroring the criticism of Ed Miliband when he was seen to be challenging Ruth Davidson, the *Express* argued that Brown criticising the Conservatives played 'right into the hands of the separatists and their skewed bid to frame the referendum as a re-run of the battles over

Thatcher's industrial policy and the poll tax', further asserting: 'That suits Labour as it airbrushes out the fact that the spendthrift Blair/Brown government brought this country to the very brink of economic ruin'.[75] The *Mail* also criticised Brown's public opinions regarding the Conservatives, though in gentler terms:

> Former Prime Minister Gordon Brown is being less than helpful by appearing to blame the Conservatives for the closeness of the vote [...] A more convincing argument for the narrowing of opinion is his own party's failure to galvanise its own traditional supporters.[76]

Brown's past record in government would also draw criticism from some commentators, even if his contemporary speeches gained near universal praise. The bulk of such critique lay in Brown's handling of the financial crisis, with several outputs laying at least part of the blame at Brown's door:

> And, if you want uncertainty, remember that the British Treasury (that's you Gordon Brown and Alistair Darling) were ignorant of what was really going on in the financial system under their stewardship even a few weeks before the first signs of collapse.[77]

Brown's failings in government provoked particular attention from the letters pages; with one submission to the *Scotsman* noting how 'Gordon Brown almost led us into economic oblivion', while a letter in the *Express* added: 'I would just like to point out [...] that the large vote for the SNP [in 2011] was more to do with the fact that we had the worst Prime Minister in living memory in No. 10'.[78] Another letter in the same title, describing Brown as 'the most disillusioned man on the planet', went on to brand the Labour backbencher as 'the man who singlehandedly almost bankrupted the UK'.[79] Given Brown's previous unpopularity with several newspaper titles, it is of note that few editorials or comment pieces from the referendum period were ever overtly critical of the former Prime Minister, though this is perhaps unsurprising, given that the majority of the press was pro-Union and Brown had emerged as the key voice articulating the desirability of such a result. One of the few instances of criticism came from Andrew Nicoll, who pointed out the evident limitations of Brown's promises regarding further devolution: 'He's not even in the party of Government. Brown is a backbench Labour MP and is not in any position to dictate the business of the House of Commons'.[80]

Taken as a whole, the press treatment of Brown's role in the referendum process is highly revealing. For one, it demonstrates that the political alignments and alliances of the newspaper industry, often thought firmly entrenched, can be rather flexible, as and when dictated by political necessity. As the coverage of Brown illustrates, even someone who has been publicly ridiculed, criticised, demonised or satirised for several years can, if working towards the correct agenda, regain a level of public relevance which might have been typically expected to elude such an individual. Gordon Brown was thus, in many ways, the right man, with the right credentials, at the right time. Despite being a Labour grandee, the pro-Conservative press were largely content to take an 'enemy of my enemy' approach to Brown's late arrival to the debate, with several titles historically hostile to all things Labour suddenly happy to endorse the ability and vision of the former Prime Minister. Such a ceasefire was also extended to include Alistair Darling, who received his fair share of positive coverage throughout the referendum campaign, despite being himself pilloried in the press for several years preceding the emergence of the independence question. The centre-right press had their limits, however, and it was notable that Ed Miliband – Labour leader in 2014 – was given far more critical treatment than other Labour colleagues. This can be partly explained through reference to the timing of the referendum: taking place less than a year before the next general election, the centre-right titles did not wish to positively publicise Miliband's role in the referendum in case such an intervention could be electorally beneficial to both himself and the Labour Party in general. Such fears did not apply to Brown, and so the Conservative-leaning press were essentially given a free hit; Brown could be lionised as a temporary titan of British politics in his defence of the Union, without his resulting increased popularity and profile expected to be a threat in the upcoming election.

Notes

1 Editorial, "Labour Pains", *Times*, 4.9.14, p. 32.
2 John McTernan, "Labour can be driving force that preserves the Union", *Scotsman*, 5.9.14, p. 24.
3 Simon Johnson, "Deal on extra powers by end of the year", *Telegraph*, 9.9.14, p. 1.
4 Editorial, "Salmond's bizarre Mandela delusion", *Mail*, 10.9.14, p. 14.
5 Dennis Urquhart, "Damaging debate", *Scotsman*, 14.8.14, p. 30.
6 Kate Devlin, "Tartan love-bombs flying right, left and centre", *Herald*, 11.9.14, p. 5.
7 Chris Musson, "Buffer Together", *Sun*, 11.9.14, p. 1.

8 Alan Roden, "Someone turns off the noisy tap as Murphy gets back on the road", *Mail*, 3.9.14, p. 9.

9 Kerry Gill, "Gordon Brown may become Scotland's most unlikely hero", *Express*, 10.9.14, p. 12.

10 Alan Cochrane, "Keep saying it: Alex Salmond's economy won't work", *Telegraph*, 3.9.14, p. 7.

11 Andrew Nicoll & Chris Musson, "Ed Nos Day", *Sun*, 5.9.14, p. 8.

12 Alan Cochrane, "Miliband opens rift in campaign to save Union", 5.9.14, p. 1.

13 Editorial, "Ed scratcher", *Sun*, 5.9.14, p. 10.

14 Editorial, "Labour pains", *Times*, 4.9.14, p. 32.

15 Pierce, "Moment Red Ed's hopes".

16 Jenni Russell, "Labour ignores the English question at its peril", *Times*, 25.9.14, p. 28.

17 Alan Roden, "Darling pleads with parents to vote No", *Mail*, 2.9.14, p. 13.

18 Hamish Macdonell, "Better Together condemned over Darling's 'common sense' posters", *Times*, 2.9.14, p. 8.

19 Alistair Darling, "This is our only chance to save the UK. We have to seize it", *Mail*, 17.9.14, p. 15.

20 Alistair Darling, "Why a No vote can bring change to Scotland, without taking a leap into the unknown", *Scotsman*, 18.9.14, p. 7.

21 David Clegg & Craig Robertson, "The cold alliance", *Record*, 27.8.14, p. 1.

22 Lindsay McIntosh, "Brown stands up for Darling", *Times*, 27.8.14, p. 1.

23 McIntosh, "Brown and Darling reunite"; For example: Simon Johnson, "Brown fears poverty until doomsday after vote for separation", *Telegraph*, 28.9.14, p. 8.

24 Magnus Gardham, "Together again as Brown and Darling cosy up for No rally", *Herald*, 28.8.14, p. 6.

25 Pike, *Project* Fear, p. 92.

26 Tom Peterkin, "Salmond and Darling in head-to-head battle", *Scotsman*, 6.8.14, p. 1.

27 Lindsay McIntosh, "First round to Darling as Salmond comes unstuck", *Times*, 6.8.14, p. 1.

28 Editorial, "Dry Alistair leaves his opponent in the dust", *Mail*, 7.8.14, p. 14.

29 Magnus Linklater, "The unexpected Mr Angry seizes his moment to attack", *Times*, 6.7.14, p. 9.

30 Alan Roden, "A bloody nose for Salmond", *Mail*, 6.8.14, p. 1; Editorial, "Rivals quick on the draw", *Sun*, 6.8.14, p. 6.

31 Alan Cochrane, "Void at heart of SNP's plan laid bare for all to see", *Telegraph*, 6.8.14, p. 3.

32 Alex Massie, "Rarely has Mr Salmond been beaten up so badly on live TV", *Times*, 6.8.14, p. 9; Alex Massie, "Was this the night dominant Mr Darling secured the Union?", *Mail*, 7.8.14, p. 14.

33 Brian Farish, "PM Brown gave SNP an election win", *Express*, 8.8.14, p. 29.

34 R Burns, "Alistair was not always the Darling of the press", *Express*, 11.8.14, p. 26.

35 Editorial, "Alex wins it on points", *Sun*, 26.8.14, p. 6.

36 Bill Leckie, "Not Salm with a plan B this time", *Sun*, 26.8.14, p. 7.

37 Philo, "Salmond won the plaudits".

38 Graham Grant, "Egg on shirt...or egg on face? How politicians fared in battle", *Mail*, 19.9.14, p. 8.

39 Gordon Kennedy, "Citizenship scandal", *Mail*, 6.8.14, p. 54.

40 Pike, *Project Fear*, p. 129.

41 Sam Coates & Lindsay McIntosh, "Brown leads Union fight after new poll shock", *The Times*, 9.9.14, p. 1.

42 Editorial, "Brown's vision is key to the Union", *Record*, 10.9.14, p. 10.

43 Mary Riddell, "Gordon: The Great Redeemer", *Telegraph*, 10.9.14, p. 17.

44 David Clegg, "Gordon's Loaded Gun", *Record*, 9.9.14, p. 2.

45 Johnson, "Deal on extra powers".

46 Gareth Rose, "'Home Rule Bill' starts the day after a No vote", *Mail*, 9.9.14, p. 10; See also: Andrew Whitaker, "Voting No 'will be starting gun for more Scots powers'", *Scotsman*, 9.9.14, pp. 6–7.

47 Editorial, "Former PM nails Salmond lies on the future of NHS", *Express*, 10.9.14, p. 12.

48 Pike, *Project Fear*, p. 133.

49 Torcuil Crichton, "Thurs Oct 16...Devo Day", *Record*, 15.9.14, p. 8.

50 George Kerevan, "Panic, cynicism and desperation", *Scotsman*, 10.9.14, p. 25.

51 Editorial, "Out of Gord-er", *Sun*, 9.9.14, p. 8.

52 Torcuil Crichton, "Brown the enforcer", *Record*, 20.9.14, p. 13.

53 Andrew Nicoll, "Labour suffer at the Hand of Gord", *Sun*, 22.9.14, p. 6.

54 Joyce McMillan, "No vote could easily be read as a triumph of fear over common sense", *Scotsman*, 20.9.14, p. 34.

55 David Clegg, "A vow can't be casually rewritten or revised", *Record*, 1.10.14, p. 6.

56 Andrew Nicoll, "It looks like we're in for a big let-down", *Sun*, 1.10.14, p. 9.

57 Torcuil Crichton, "Division and inequality will be Salmond legacy", *Record*, 11.9.14, p. 10; David Clegg, "I'll be back", *Record*, 12.9.14, p. 10.

58 Editorial, "Brown's vision".

59 Kerry Gill, "Gordon Brown may become Scotland's most unlikely hero", *Express*, 10.9.14, p. 12.

60 Riddell, "Gordon: The Great Redeemer".

61 Gareth Rose, "Brown close to tears as he salutes NHS team that tried to save his girl", *Mail*, 10.9.14, p. 9.

62 Quentin Letts, "Shrivelled tomato? No, Brown is back", *Mail*, 9.9.14, p. 10.

63 Alan Cochrane, "The Nats' NHS lie is the biggest"; Alan Cochrane, "New deal gets its ideal messenger", *Telegraph*, 9.9.14, p. 4.

64 Alan Roden, "Spin, vitriol and the bitter war of words fought to win your votes", *Mail*, 18.9.14, p. 12.

65 Andrew Whitaker, "Brown urges Scots 'hold your head high' and vote No", *Scotsman*, 18.9.14, p. 9; Gordon Tait, "The word of Gord", *Sun*, 18.9.14, p. 6.

66 Lindsay McIntosh, "Brown comes alive with a blast of passion and fury", *Times*, 18.9.14, p. 7.

67 Andrew Whitaker, "Labour's big beasts 'hauled No camp back from the brink'", *Scotsman*, 20.9.14, p. 10.

68 Grant, "Egg on shirt".

69 Ann Treneman, "Less Mickey Mouse now, more a wee, timorous beastie", *Times*, 20.9.14, p. 7; David McMillan, "SNP should now accept that No must mean No for a generation", *Herald*, 20.9.14, p. 18.

70 Paul Ward, "Brown: I'll be back to take on Salmond", *Sun*, 12.9.14, p. 6; Clegg, "I'll be back".

71 Alan Roden & Gareth Rose, "Bruiser Brown promises to take the fight to Holyrood as he goes to war for the NHS", *Mail*, 12.9.14, p. 8.

72 Kerry Gill, "Salmond's parting gift: Proof Scots got it right", *Express*, 20.9.14, p. 12.

73 Editorial, "Brown could end strife of the Salmond years", *Express*, 22.9.14, p. 12.

74 Grant, "Egg on shirt".

75 Editorial, "Labour's late show", *Mail*, 4.9.14, p. 14.

76 Editorial, "No camp has to pull out stops to defeat Salmond", *Express*, 8.9.14.

77 Isobel Lindsay, "Women will pay a heavy price if they gamble on voting No", *Herald*, 13.8.14, p. 14.

78 Alan Black, "No voter myth", *Scotsman*, 25.9.14, p. 32; Davy Martin, "PM Brown gave SNP an election win", *Express*, 8.8.14, p. 29.

79 Niall McGlone, "We don't need lectures from Brown and Obama", *Express*, 18.9.14, p. 25.

80 Nicoll, "Labour suffer".

7   Eck of a story
The focus on Alex Salmond

Though the campaign to retain Scotland's place in the Union had a variety of champions – David Cameron, the Queen, Alistair Darling and Gordon Brown being the main personalities in this regard – the Yes campaign was presented and framed, on the whole, with reference to one man: Scotland's First Minister at the time, Alex Salmond. Not all of the coverage dedicated to Salmond was negative, despite many titles being explicitly pro-Union, but it remained the case that press coverage of the referendum generally presented independence as synonymous with the First Minister. Indeed, the extent of this can be appreciated by even a cursory glance at the footnotes informing this chapter, with Salmond's name dominating the headlines to an extent unmatched by any other individual.

Every move you make: criticism of Salmond

Generating more personal coverage than anyone else involved in the referendum debate, in a media landscape which was mostly pro-Unionist, Alex Salmond predictably came in for consistent criticism throughout the period leading to the vote. Aspects of Salmond's personality, political style and plans for an independent Scotland were endlessly dissected and critiqued, in a manner which was, rather tellingly, not repeated for those representing the No campaign. This continued even after Salmond announced he was to stand down, with the decision to exclude those representing the *Telegraph*, *Mail*, *Financial Times* and *Express* from attending the resignation address drawing comment from the latter's Kerry Gill: 'A petty, vindictive, final retaliation against the three media organisations that had done so much to stymie his plans to break up the United Kingdom. It could be taken as a compliment, but it certainly wasn't meant as such'.[1] In terms of criticising Salmond directly, the *Mail* was something of a stand-out,

DOI: 10.4324/9781003138259-7

with various commentators and other journalists framing the First Minister in generally unflattering terms. 'He can be awkward around women and even rude at times, as though he never quite knows how to handle something as complicated as female company', noted Emma Cowing,

> he can also appear remarkably thin-skinned – unable to take criticism and lashing out at those who target him [...] Even in social situations it is as if sometimes he's waiting to be told when to be told when to laugh at a joke.[2]

Other columnists for the *Mail* drew further attention to Salmond's perceived faults, with his debating style, manner of public engagement and relationship with journalists all being commonly cited as weaknesses. These same criticisms would, however, often be mentioned alongside an (often begrudging) appreciation for the First Minister's talents. As Quentin Letts would write:

> The way he had energised the under-30s and non-professionals in the campaign was remarkable. If only he had managed to do so while giving straight answers. If only he had not betrayed acid resentment every time an English man, or more particularly woman, asked him a question.[3]

Arguing that the First Minister's 'unsurpassable confidence in his own ability' had 'often been a source of strength and cheer for the SNP', Alex Massie would go on to warn, just before the second debate with Darling, that 'you can have too much of a good thing and Mr Salmond's swagger now seems to repel as many voters as it attracts'.[4] Such criticisms would also find voice among the letters published in the *Mail*, with Salmond a favourite topic for discussion in this forum. With the author citing the fact that his father's generation 'fought against nationalism again in 1940–45', one submission would assert, 'Our home is not a football to be kicked around by second-rate politicians to satisfy their egos'.[5]

A related though important aspect of this negative coverage of Alex Salmond was that which presented the First Minister as being untrustworthy or otherwise unreliable. Given the supposed emphasis placed on facts being central to an informed decision as to how to vote, presenting the key messenger of the pro-independence campaign as being an inherently untrustworthy individual becomes crucial to understanding the key framing devices used by the pro-Unionist titles;

particularly when compared to the coverage of No campaign representatives, whose claims and counter-positions – though usually as speculative in nature as those emanating from the opposing side – were rarely subjected to the level of interrogation or critique directed at seemingly every intervention by Alex Salmond or the wider Yes campaign. A frequent point of contention was that the SNP's plans, as set out in the White Paper published in November 2013, were little more than fantasy, with Salmond's proposals for an independent Scotland invariably defined as un-costed, unrealistic or otherwise unworkable. 'I'm starting to suspect a consequence of this referendum could be the fatal undermining of Mr Salmond's authority: it could yet prove to be his Wizard of Oz moment', opined Chris Deerin, 'The fearsome wizard is, like all great conjuring acts, just a bloke with delusions of grandeur. There is no such thing as magic'.[6] This theme would be echoed by Alan Cochrane, who called on the No campaign to reemphasise the message 'that separation equals, not the nirvana that Alex Salmond promises and cannot deliver, but only risk and doubt'.[7]

That Salmond could be short or evasive with sections of the media was also commented upon, which perhaps helped to underscore the idea that Salmond was usually less-than-straightforward with Scotland's electorate. In one instance, having 'abandoned any pretence of being an international statesman', as Alan Roden would report for the *Mail* about a particular media gathering, Salmond was described as having 'presided over an astonishing press conference in which he was tetchy, rattled and – according to several observers – "losing the plot"'.[8] Of the same event, Alan Cochrane – highlighting, 'Those of us who deal with him on a regular basis know full well that this hail-fellow-well-met cheery chappie who's been back-slapping his way around Scotland for the last 10 days is not exactly the real Alex' – would go on to opine, 'it was only a matter of time before the impostor [...] gave way to the entirely different character that the journalists who have to report on his doings [...] would recognise'.[9] Indeed, the trustworthiness of Alex Salmond and the veracity of his claims were a recurring target for Cochrane, at various junctures. 'Unfortunately for them, but fortunately for me and those who support Better Together, they're stuck with him', remarked Cochrane,

> stuck with his Project Fib, stuck with his half-truths, stuck with downright deceptions [...] and above all stuck with his determination to save his political career by winning the referendum by insisting that he's right and everyone else is wrong.[10]

Commentary in the *Sun* repeated similar themes, though placed a different emphasis on the issue of trust as it applied to Salmond and the electorate. 'But [independence] might be difficult. It could be hard. We might suffer', accepted Andrew Nicoll, 'And those are the words Alex Salmond has never trusted us enough to utter. He has never been able to say that, like any prize worth winning, independence might come at a price'.[11]

Indeed, this issue regarding Salmond's ability to be trusted, although common in the press throughout the referendum period, arguably peaked in the days immediately following the first televised debate with Alistair Darling. In an exchange which the Better Together leader was widely judged to have won, Salmond's weaker discussion of currency options received extensive press attention, with this public failure often framed as further evidence of Salmond's untrustworthiness. 'Salmond had had months to prepare a suitable response. But he was caught napping in his TV debate with Alistair Darling', asserted a *Record* editorial, 'Salmond now faces a monumental task to reassure Scots that their money will be secure after a Yes vote'.[12] Writing in the *Sun*, Bill Leckie remarked that the debate had 'called for the witty, engaging, conciliatory Alex Salmond to stand up', lamenting that 'he'd been locked up in a cupboard Scooby-Doo style by the smug, shifty, second-hand car-dealer alter ego the First Minister can't help himself from becoming when handed the chance to showboat'.[13] While highlighting that Salmond had been 'Scotland's most able and charismatic politician of the last decade [...] But his surefooted instinct has deserted him just when it matters most', a *Sun* editorial also linked Salmond's less-assured first debate performance to the prospects for an independent Scotland. 'It's not just bad news for him – it's a blow for the whole country. With the big vote less than six weeks away, Scots deserve a better fight than this', continued the lead article, 'Independence should be decided on ALL the issues – not left to wither away on Mr Salmond's stubbornness'.[14]

Though often presented as personally unlikable, politically untrustworthy or otherwise less than forthcoming with the Scottish electorate, Alex Salmond would also be explicitly linked to small and infrequent instances of abuse or harassment seen to be emanating from the pro-independence campaign. Violence or intimidation of a serious order was notable during the referendum campaign for its general absence, a rather remarkable observation when one considers the potential magnitude of the constitutional issue at stake, in addition to favourably comparing Scotland's referendum process with myriad more violent or chaotic instances around the world where similar issues have been in the balance. Nonetheless, unsavoury aspects of modern political discourse were regularly placed at Salmond's door, with the figurehead of the Yes campaign often framed as being somehow responsible for the actions of a minority, whether that be heckling of candidates, the defacement of political posters or the actions of online trolls.

Perhaps the key case study of this particular trend was that concerning the street-campaigning tour of Labour MP, Jim Murphy. Murphy's own claims of being a victim of organised harassment – often implying that the SNP leader was in some way directly connected to, for example, the throwing of eggs on a Kirkcaldy street – were either uncontested by the press or used to argue that Salmond's leadership was directing, or otherwise responsible for, a series of quasi-violent organised actions. Though in light of, for example, the murder of MP Jo Cox or the storming of the US Capitol, the skirmishes and confrontations of Scotland's referendum debate seem rather paltry by comparison, the supposed harassment of Jim Murphy generated considerable coverage from a number of press outlets. The *Telegraph*, in particular, drew regular attention to this feature of the debate, often directly framing the actions against Murphy as resulting from top-level SNP direction. Reporting after Salmond's poor showing in the first televised debate, a front page *Telegraph* article cited how Murphy 'no longer encountered pro-Salmond hecklers and that there was a "crisis of confidence" in the First Minister'.[15] Following his pelting with eggs in a Kirkcaldy shopping precinct, which led to a short-lived suspension of Murphy's tour, the Labour MP would also be quoted, quite uncritically, about his thoughts regarding the origins of such incidents. 'The former Scottish Secretary said he did not know whether Alex Salmond was responsible for the respite after the First Minister used a television interview at the weekend to urge people to ignore him', reported Simon Johnson, 'Asked whether the mobs had listened to Mr Salmond's advice, Mr Murphy said: "Whoever turned on that noisy tap of aggressive political behaviour has quietly turned it off again".[16] The *Times* also covered the story in such a manner; arguably giving further credence to the idea that the First Minister, in the middle of the intense final weeks of an unprecedented political campaign over Scotland's future, had somehow found both the time and inclination to conceive of and organise a series of small-scale interventions with the ultimate intention of disrupting Jim Murphy standing on an Irn-Bru crate. 'Alex Salmond was at the centre of a row over campaign bullying yesterday when he was criticised for refusing to take a hard line on the "mob" of Yes Scotland supporters who harass their opponents', noted one news article, going on to report how Murphy had been 'forced to suspend a countrywide speaking tour last week because of an orchestrated campaign of abuse against him by independence supporters in towns across the country'.[17]

That Salmond was perceived as stirring up resentment or encouraging such behaviour, in both Scotland and the rest of the United Kingdom, remained a feature throughout the coverage, as illustrated by a letter submitted to the *Scotsman* threating, 'The First Minister seems anxious to promote as much distrust and ill-feeling south of the Border as he can'.[18] Some contributors actively developed the notion of Salmond (even implicitly) condoning the misdeeds of a minority of Yes supporters; such as when Michael Deacon, reporting on Salmond's response to being asked why he attracted 'these abusive people', reported: 'Silently, Mr Salmond turned his back on me, and directed his answer to a journalist standing on the opposite side of the huddle'.[19] Brian Monteith, writing in the *Scotsman*, would be among the more direct with such accusations, however:

> It has been brewing for a long time, since last May in fact, but finally we are seeing the threat of violence and intimidation sour the independence referendum – and the First Minister must take a large share of the responsibility for this.

Monteith would further insist that 'the blame for this bitter and ugly mood goes right to the top, beyond the Yes campaign staff, to the First Minister', before contextualising his remarks somewhat,

> not because [Salmond] is organising it or knows any of the people behind it – but because when this mobbing and threatening behaviour began last year with the visit of Nigel Farage to Edinburgh, he failed to condemn it in the strongest possible terms.[20]

A few minor exceptions emerged in the discussion of Salmond's supposed involvement with the darker edges of the wider Yes campaign, however, with some commentators noting that the First Minister's alleged role in such actions had arguably been overstated (while not entirely rejecting the idea, either): 'It was even hinted at – unfairly perhaps – that the notorious cybernats and the Yes campaign's over-aggressive street campaigners were formed in the image of their party leader'.[21] Others pointed to the double-standards at play, at least in terms of highlighting – and arguably exaggerating – seemingly every instance of foul-play or supposed intimidation coming from either

Salmond or the Yes campaign. 'There would, I'm pretty certain, be an extended, quivering, self-righteous orgy of over-the-top condemnation. Indeed, I reckon ordinary Scots would be led to believe the very basis of our civilization was under extreme threat', commented Harry Reid, speculating on the hysteria that would follow a hypothetical scenario where Alex Salmond punched someone: 'The rhetoric from the likes of Jim Murphy would no doubt take indignation to a sublime pitch that I can hardly imagine'.[22]

Notable in the press criticism of Alex Salmond, in many ways built on the foundations of the media image of him being both personally unlikable and in some way encouraging 'mob violence', was the persistent framing of the First Minister as displaying dictatorial tendencies. In a manner which was never replicated for any of the big-name politicos involved in the No campaign, Salmond was regularly portrayed as being authoritarian, admiring totalitarian regimes or having ambitions towards establishing some kind of dictatorship in an undefined possible future. One of the more direct reports came from the *Express*, which quoted the words of Tory MSP, Alex Johnstone: 'Alex Salmond was accused of behaving like a "dictator" yesterday [...] "Perhaps his dislike for scrutiny and fury at anyone who dares to question his grand vision are what attracted the North Korean regime to Scottish independence"'.[23] Indeed, North Korea's alleged support for Scottish independence (though no official statement to this effect had actually been released) made a few appearances in the coverage, often framed as being indicative in some way of Salmond's authoritarian sympathies. The *Mail* reported how 'after warnings by Barack Obama, Hilary Clinton and Pope Francis against separation, Alex Salmond has at last received a high-profile international endorsement – from North Korea'.[24] An *Express* editorial would further reference other regimes and groups to establish some sort of tenuous link to Salmond and his plans for an independent Scotland: 'there was a moment of farce yesterday when North Korea said it favoured a Yes vote. Alex Salmond's hoped for split with the United Kingdom has also been backed by Russian separatists in the Ukraine. With friends like these...'. The same lead article further noted how a press conference had offered 'a glimpse of the kind of state Alex Salmond would run. A normally sober press conference had clearly been packed with SNP and Yes supporters who applauded Mr Salmond's ill-tempered attempt to silence Nick Robinson of the BBC', concluding that, 'Perhaps the backing of North Korea and Russian-backed separatists had lent Mr Salmond some encouragement'.[25]

Other commentary lent credibility to the idea of Salmond as a kind of potential dictator, some of which explicitly likened the First Minister to tyrannical figures of the past. Recounting how he was informed that Salmond supposedly does not apply his own personal disinfectant – 'An accompanying flunkey whipped out some hand sanitiser and reverently smeared it on to the sacred mitts of power' – Chris Deerin would question: 'Is King Eck going a bit Louis XIV?'[26] Opining on other comments by Salmond, which had clumsily likened Scotland's referendum with South Africa's first free democratic vote in 1994, the *Telegraph* did not hold back in its criticism. 'If the First Minister was seeking to portray himself as the equivalent of Nelson Mandela, perhaps there is another African leader who springs more readily to mind: Robert Mugabe', noted the editorial, 'Mr Salmond's skills are in reaping division and sowing discord. He might also, like the Zimbabwean leader, be about to drag his country into an economic calamity'.[27] Taking a different approach, but nonetheless framing Salmond as having ambitions towards being regarded as something of a contemporary historical icon, the *Mail* was also critical of the First Minister's invocation of the South African example: 'With break-taking legerdemain, Alex Salmond likens Scots to black South Africans emerging from the Apartheid era – presumably casting himself in the role of Nelson Mandela. How preposterous'.[28] Not every description of Salmond cast him in a dictatorial or otherwise cult-of-personality light, however, with others drawing more subtle attention to his political ideals or philosophies. As Emma Cowing noted, 'His recent blunder that he admired Russian President Vladimir Putin would suggest that as he approaches his 60th birthday, there is still a part of him that still strolls around in a Maoist cap set at a jaunty angle'.[29] Continuing this trend, David Aaronovitch would make reference to, 'Salmondism, in which no difficult choices are made, almost nothing is actually altered – not the Queen, taxes, currency or property – yet everything is somehow different'.[30]

The manner in which Salmond both controlled his party and drew public adulation from sections of his own support was also remarked upon, in a way which also strengthened this authoritarian characterisation of the First Minister. For example, reporting on 'a private pep talk intended to boost their morale', a front page *Scotsman* headline would declare, *Salmond orders his party: 'Go out and win'*. An earlier *Express* article, on the other hand, instead argued that Salmond's leadership was under scrutiny following his first debate defeat: 'today, the First Minister is a man without a plan, a leader on the ropes, the subject of deep unease within his own party'.[31] Certainly, speculating on the apparent authoritarian tendencies of both Salmond and the SNP found voice in several outlets, with many describing what were seen as cult-like tendencies. 'Throughout the campaign the separatists – the magnificently untameable Jim Sillars aside – have maintained a discipline bordering on the creepy', observed Chris Deerin, 'Ironically, their obsession with independence seems to have removed the capability of independent thought'.[32] It should be stressed though that not all of this coverage was necessarily negative, with Salmond's political star, on occasion, highlighted as being evidently undeniable. David Clegg, reporting how Salmond 'was treated like a superstar as he hit the campaign trail yesterday', would go on to illustrate the First Minister's popularity, citing that Salmond had 'posed for selfies with more than 100 well-wishers'; while Quentin Letts, commenting on the level of public engagement from the SNP leader, would describe: 'Salmondistas held little signs saying "Yes" to independence in various languages'.[33]

All the same, language which presented both Salmond and the Yes campaign as having fascistic or dictatorial ideals – though sparingly used – remained a notable feature of the discourse surrounding the referendum. The alleged nature of Yes supporters was often cited in support of this idea, such as in the following guest column by Archie MacPherson: 'This was simply fever, red-necked, red-faced raw hatred that has been induced by those in the Yes camp who are ceaselessly affronted by contradictions to their own views'.[34] A comment piece in the *Mail* described how Salmond had been 'accompanied by marvellous heavies, straight from Bodyguard Central Casting, necks as thick as birch trees and dressed in those shiny, black suits', drawing a direct comparison to the leader of UKIP: 'Nigel Farage employs similar hired meat – this year's must-have item for nationalist demagogues, perhaps'.[35] Such themes would be echoed in a report from the *Herald*, detailing the concerns of writer Ewan Morrison, who had switched from Yes to No after seeing the independence campaign as 'self-censoring, conformist and cult-like'.[36] Other contributions, with particular frequency in the days immediately surrounding the vote itself, threated over the type of political regime which could hypothetically emerge in an independent Scotland. 'We witnessed quiet, eloquent democracy on September 18', opined a letter to the *Mail*, 'the SNP now shows its true colours by shouting loudly to smother it'.[37] Writing after the result had been secured, Kerry Gill would comment that the banning of various newspapers from Salmond's resignation speech was indicative of the kind of future that might have awaited

Scotland: 'That three of Britain's leading newspapers were banned from Mr Salmond's last press conference perhaps tells us the direction an independent Scotland would have taken. A frightening glimpse of the authoritarian state that we have so narrowly escaped'.[38] A letter appearing in the same title advised, 'Perhaps the undecided voters should heed George Orwell's Animal Farm', reminding readers that, 'as time passes, the animals realise that conditions are no better than before – indeed, in some respects they are worse'.[39]

As expected, with a largely pro-Unionist press, much of the coverage of Alex Salmond – both in terms of his claims regarding independence and of the First Minister personally – was demonstrably negative. The SNP leader was painted in various unflattering colours, in a manner not replicated to the same degree for political heavyweights from the No campaign, such as David Cameron or Gordon Brown. There were some notable (brief) exceptions to this trend, however, with Salmond coming in for short-lived but concentrated positive coverage. One such instance came in the days immediately following the second televised debate with Alistair Darling, in which Salmond was generally adjudged to have emerged the victor. Describing a 'dramatic, aggressive comeback' during which 'the first minister put in a far more confident, pugilistic performance', Lindsay McIntosh of the *Times* emphasised the fact that Salmond had apparently risen to the occasion, after his weaker showing in the first outing: 'It was his chance to make the case for his independence dream directly to hundreds of thousands of voters in their own living rooms – and he seized it with both hands'.[40] The *Sun* would repeat such praise, asserting that Salmond had been 'Well prepared, quick on his feet, commanding, a man sure of his case and confident of victory', stressing the dominance of his debate triumph in further sporting terms: 'If it had been a boxing match they'd have thrown in the towel long before the finish'.[41] At no other point in the coverage, however, was praise for Salmond anywhere near as unanimous nor wide-ranging as that which followed the announcement of his resignation, which, for one day at least, bordered on the Diana-esque.

King for a day: praise for Salmond

Newspaper coverage from Saturday 20 September was notable for two reasons, in that these were the first editions to cover both the definitive result of the referendum and the resignation of Alex Salmond as First Minister. Though these events were of course publicised through broadcast and online media as they first emerged the day prior, the print media were only in a position to address such developments afterwards. Salmond's resignation thus came to be the key framing device in presenting the outcome of the referendum, with the result itself gaining secondary coverage. Salmond's decision came to dominate the front pages and editorial columns of virtually every newspaper, with a persistent feature of the coverage being the presentation of independence as a personal vision of Salmond. 'Alex Salmond dramatically resigned [...] after Scots rejected his dream of independence', noted a page one article in the *Mail*, mirroring similar language in the *Scotsman*: 'Alex Salmond has resigned as Scotland's First Minister after his lifelong dream of an independent Scotland was rejected by the people'.[42] This concept was further emphasised in the front page headlines of the *Record* and the *Times*, which, respectively, reported *The dream shall never die* and *END OF A DREAM*; both being accompanied by solemn-looking pictures of the soon-to-be ex-First Minister.[43] Much of the coverage also stressed the fact that Salmond's resignation had been largely unpredicted, with his decision to step down apparently taking many within the press by surprise. As Magnus Gardham of the *Herald* would report: 'The SNP leader yesterday stunned the political world by deciding to resign within hours of failing to realise his dream of leading Scotland to independence'.[44] Coverage from the *Times* meanwhile noted how Salmond's resignation had 'stunned the country [...] less than 12 hours after Scots rejected his independence plan'.[45] This is not to say, however, that there were not also examples of the resignation being covered with a less reverential tone. Indeed, some commentators saw his decision as inevitable, given the majority for No. 'In a rare example of personal insight, Mr Salmond realised that he was yesterday's man', commented Kerry Gill, 'That there was no way the public would take him as seriously as he took himself anymore. His era had come to an end'.[46] Quentin Letts repeated similar ideas, though in more creative language: 'On the fishmonger's marble slab, one Salmond, gutted. He had fought a long, strong campaign, giving those hated "Southerners" a mighty onset of the collywobbles. But he had lost and it was not entirely a surprise that he quit'.[47]

Despite the occasional dissenting voice, however, coverage from 20 September was quite exceptional in the degree of positive coverage afforded Salmond; a trend which was at odds with the general tone of press treatment of the First Minister to that point. Even in those explicitly pro-Unionist, Conservative titles which devoted considerable time and energy to critiquing every aspect of Salmond, the SNP or the wider Yes campaign, the First Minister's resignation proved the catalyst for a sudden outpouring of praise for the SNP leader. One may read this positive framing of Salmond as, in part, resulting from a feeling of relief on the part of many in the press; with the desired result secured *and* Salmond soon to relinquish the leadership, praising him to any particular degree thus came with far less political risk. Nonetheless, even with such a cynical reading as this, the coverage from this immediate post-resignation period remains interesting for its dramatic shift in tone.

A key aspect of this positive framing of Salmond and his legacy was the emphasis placed on his undeniable role in Scotland having taken part in a referendum in the first place. In other words, Salmond was seen as responsible for providing Scotland with the opportunity to debate, and ultimately vote on, an issue which was surely of great political importance. 'They may not like [Salmond] or his policies, but they appreciate that he has given them the chance to decide, one way or the other, an issue that goes to the heart of the nation', opined Magnus Linklater, 'It is a debate that Scotland had to have. It has informed and enlightened the people. It has cleared the air'.[48] Emphasising similar themes, Ian Bell would write, 'Were it not for Alex Salmond, we would not have had a plebiscite on self-determination'. Writing for the *Herald*, Bell was explicit in his gratitude for the impact the general referendum campaign had had on Scotland's concept of itself: '[Salmond] has done more than any in my Scottish generation to think – for he's good at that – about what independence can mean for a small country in a big world'.[49] Such praise for Salmond would also appear in submissions to the letters pages, some of which even emerged prior to his decision to resign: 'No matter what the outcome in two weeks, we can all be proud Alex Salmond, Nicola Sturgeon and their team reinvigorated politics like no other before them'.[50]

Beyond his role in making independence a key issue in Scottish politics, others drew specific attention to Salmond's impact on the electoral fortunes of his party. 'When he first became SNP leader (for the first time) in 1990, few accepted the economic viability of an independent Scotland', commented David Torrance, 'nearly a quarter of a century later even ardent unionists reluctantly conceded the possibility (if not the desirability) of a separate Scottish state'. In a separate column for the *Scotsman*, Torrance would continue: 'What of his legacy? Making independence not only credible but possible, indeed tantalisingly [...] That he didn't succeed almost doesn't matter, for he has left so much for his successor to take forward'.[51] Such language would be utilised in the *Record*, with David Clegg highlighting that Salmond's career 'took the cause of Scottish nationalism to unimaginable victories'.[52]

Also highlighted by several contributors was Salmond's influence on the wider British political scene, with the SNP leader framed as something of a maverick who had shaken the foundations of British party politics. An editorial in the *Herald* would argue that Salmond had 'spent his political life defying lazy or patronising assumptions, especially those of complacent Westminster politicians', a theme continued by Andy Philip: 'The supercharged referendum debate proved Salmond was a global player, and he got close enough to victory to scare the Westminster parties into promising to work urgently to give major new powers to Scotland'.[53] The *Mail* also joined this chorus of praise, describing Salmond's commitment to the campaign as 'at times, awe-inspiring' and offering the following assessment: 'In truth, it is highly unlikely anyone but this man could have led the SNP into government, far less carve open the Westminster defence and set up a clear shot at goal'.[54] The 20 September editorial in the *Record*, however, is something of a standout in this regard, heaping praise on Salmond in a manner which often drifted into hyperbole. Describing the SNP leader's impact in 'turning his once small party into a political force that threatened to do nothing less than shake the western world order until the walls of the temple fell down', the editorial continued, 'No one took Alex Salmond lightly and he took on the full might of the British establishment, and nearly won'.[55]

Amidst such commentary, attention was further drawn to a range of Salmond's achievements; with the SNP leader gaining an apparent respect and adulation from the press, in defeat, which was all but denied him before the No result was secured. For example, Magnus Linklater would state, 'The campaign that Mr Salmond has just fought might go down in history as a defeat, but it is one he can be justifiably proud of', adding that Salmond had 'energised the country and engaged it in the greatest political debate of modern times'.[56] Interpreting the fact that 1.6 million voters had backed independence as 'by any standard an astonishing endorsement of this man and his achievements', the *Herald* was in agreement that such a result could only have been achieved by this particular individual: 'Such a result would probably have been inconceivable in the hands of any other leader'.[57] Again, one can interpret this sudden and concentrated outpouring of pro-Salmond opinion as only being possible given the fact that a pro-Union majority had already been confirmed. Had the result gone the other way, one can assume that several of the titles would have discussed Salmond and his legacy in infinitely more negative terms. All the same, for one day at least, Salmond was widely portrayed – in a largely uncritical manner – as a political colossus, the apparent bane of Westminster politics and a man to whom Scotland owed something of a collective democratic debt. 'As a dominant figure in modern Scottish politics, Alex Salmond is the equal of Donald Dewar. As a lightning rod for division, anger, even hatred, he is almost the equal of Margaret Thatcher', commented Andy Philip in the *Record*, 'Dewar gave us our Parliament. Salmond gave us our inspiring referendum and set the future course of Scotland – and Britain too. All Scots should be grateful to him for that'.[58]

Beyond this there was a further aspect to this brief narrative groundswell of positive coverage, with Salmond generally portrayed as having displayed a variety of positive traits both during the referendum campaign and over his longer political career. While stating that the press exhibited a fondness for the outgoing First Minister would be a stretch, commentary from the time nonetheless revealed varying degrees of respect for Salmond, with many accepting that his departure would leave an obvious void in Scottish politics. 'For nearly two decades he has bestrode the political scene, first as a thorn in the side of the Westminster establishment, then as skilful leader of a minority government, then as the First Minister who took his country to the brink of becoming a new state', editorialised the *Record*, 'We all lived through history in the last week and it was Salmond who took us there'.[59] The *Sun* mirrored such sentiments, seeing Salmond's resignation as a loss for Scotland: 'So Alex Salmond must be given credit for falling on his sword. The problem for Scotland is that the First Minister's resignation comes just when his country needs him most'.[60] Other contributors drew attention to Salmond's record in government, in addition to highlighting his unique place in the Scottish political landscape. 'Everyone said he was a dodgy character and that he would get found out. But no one ever did', commented Iain MacWhirter; with David Torrance, noting that Salmond had 'become a sort of Scottish everyman – divisive, certainly, but a politician whose ability few doubted however they viewed the broader pitch', going on to reaffirm Salmond's unique political legacy: 'He is at once a very modern politician and a figure – rhetorically, at least – from another era. Few could have balanced the two with such panache or longevity'.[61]

The First Minister's resignation also elicited comment as to how his presence would be missed, not least from those journalists accustomed to interacting with him. As Magnus Linklater recalled: 'No press conference with him was dull, no encounter took place without the faint shiver of electricity'.[62] Certainly, so widespread was this almost nostalgic response that even the *Mail*, historically hostile towards Salmond and the SNP, went on to gently praise the Yes campaign figurehead. 'Some journalists (including me) were not admitted to the resignation announcement', recalled Quentin Letts, '[...] But it would be churlish to allow that minor slight to taint the day, for the truth is that Mr Salmond, for all his faults, reached into the emotional gizzards of the electorate'.[63] The *Mail*'s 20 September editorial is an interesting example in this regard, apparently balancing a critique of Salmond with a resigned acceptance of his role both in the referendum and in wider Scottish politics. 'This newspaper has deep concerns about many aspects of SNP policy and about Mr Salmond's unwillingness to wield the axe to Cabinet dead wood', noted the lead article, 'But when he steps down as First Minister in November, Scottish politics will be a little duller'. As the editorial further opined: 'Still, we cannot forget how Mr Salmond's vainglorious dance led the country to the very brink of the independence precipice. It was, regardless of the recklessness of his policies, a bravura performance'.[64]

Of course, such an outpouring of sentiment and respect for Salmond was to be short-lived, ultimately expiring within days of his resignation. Though not the case to the same extent with titles such as the *Sun* or the *Record*, many of the right-leaning newspapers quickly resumed their criticism of the outgoing First Minister. By 22 September, both the *Express* and the *Mail*, in remarkably similar language, used their front pages to publicise the supposed threat of independence being achieved other than through the ballot box. 'Alex Salmond was last night accused of attempting to stage a "coup" after suggesting Scotland could become independent without a referendum', reported the *Express*, while the *Mail* framed Salmond's comments as 'an extraordinary display totally at odds with his defeat in the referendum'.[65] Referencing Salmond's statements regarding other routes to independence, the *Mail* confronted the issue in an editorial. 'There has been dangerous talk from Mr Salmond and many within his party [...] of "other routes" to separation. That is as demeaning for them as it is alarming for the public', noted the lead article, further warning, 'Any attempt to circumvent the referendum will simply not be tolerated'.[66]

Evidently, Salmond's moment in the sun was to last barely 24 hours for many of the newspapers concerned. It remains notable, however, that he was granted such positive coverage at all, what with the majority of the press being openly anti-independence; of course, one also has to consider the timing of such positive coverage, coming as it did once the result desired by much of the press had been secured. In other words, much in the same way that typically anti-Labour newspapers were content to praise Gordon Brown due to the limited impact of this on the upcoming 2015 election, Salmond's resignation – in combination with the No victory in the referendum – granted the press a certain freedom, in that the First Minister could be given what was seen as his just due, without the risk of such positive coverage translating into increased electoral popularity for either Salmond or his party.

Also worth highlighting, despite being rare in the coverage, were those contributions which directly engaged with the media's presentation of Salmond, variously noting that the First Minister was a more multifaceted character than the individual often caricatured in newspaper accounts. Commenting of the tone of some of the post-resignation coverage, Lesley Riddoch would wonder in the *Herald*: 'Perhaps that speaks to the fondness adversaries can suddenly feel when old rivals depart. Perhaps that's because the half-man, half-monster figure deliberately created by lacklustre political rivals was always a wild exaggeration'.[67] Indeed, Riddoch had expressed a similar view weeks before the referendum had taken place. 'Heavyweight yet slippery, possessed of wizard-like powers and a hypnotic control over many Scottish voters [...] Salmond has been transformed into a latter-day Robert the Bruce – fighting the London establishment to win control in Scotland for his own murky, greedy and nefarious ends', described Riddoch in her *Scotsman* column, 'It makes good copy. It sells papers. It gives us all a laugh. But this sinister creation isn't real. And most of the public knows it'.[68] David Torrance continued such an analysis, writing in the *Herald*:

> Personally, to paraphrase Walt Whitman, Mr Salmond was large (though that changed in recent years) and contained multitudes [...] he was a big beast, so much so it's difficult to conceive of a Scottish political stage deprived of his presence.[69]

In a *Times* piece, the same author would simply state: 'Perhaps the most important thing to understand about the first minister and leader of the SNP is that there are many different Alex Salmonds'.[70]

These latter examples were rare, however, with much of the coverage painting Salmond in a negative light, a trend that was especially evident in the likes of the *Mail*, *Express* and *Telegraph*. Though, as detailed, Salmond did receive short bursts of positive reporting, on the whole it was the case that the reverential, respectful and nostalgic coverage granted to Salmond following his resignation was something of an anomaly, and not representative of the general coverage afforded the First Minister in the weeks and months leading to the referendum.

Just a man: the personalisation of the debate

Though Salmond demonstrably became a target for regular criticism, in addition to enjoying a brief post-resignation outpouring of positive coverage, a defining feature of the news and comment dedicated to the First Minister was that he was consistently presented as being one in the same as the abstract concept of independence. In headlines, editorials and various other sections, Scottish independence was equated explicitly with Alex Salmond's version of it, to the point where personal failings and critiques of Salmond were presented as being evidence of the supposed weaknesses of the general independence project. Indeed, while the No campaign had various figureheads and spokespersons, none of these were framed as being the personification of Unionism. The pro-independence position, on the other hand, was variously presented as the personal quest of Alex Salmond, a framing device which was evident across all newspapers, but which appeared with greater regularity and emphasis in the centre-right titles taking a stronger Unionist editorial line.

There were myriad examples of this phenomenon in the reporting of the referendum, with the independence debate often being framed as a choice between the United Kingdom and Alex Salmond, as opposed to the wider constitutional issue which it clearly was. 'Alex Salmond's campaign to leave the United Kingdom needs only three more points to claim victory', noted one such article in the *Times*, repeating a trend observed throughout coverage of the Yes campaign.[71] Though perhaps expected given the format of the events, this was particularly pronounced during the televised debates with Alistair Darling, with Salmond's weaker showing in the first outing being presented as directly damaging the lure of independence. 'Alex Salmond's campaign for Scottish independence suffered a major setback last night after he lost the first referendum television debate and was booed by the audience', highlighted a front page article in the *Telegraph*, with a *Mail* editorial opining: 'The Mail fervently hopes that this debate will mark a turning point in the campaign, when those seduced by Mr Salmond's romantic rhetoric will begin to consider the realities of independence'.[72] That much of the debate had witnessed Darling focusing on Salmond himself, as opposed to critiquing other policy issues beyond currency, prompted comment from Alex Massie. Highlighting how Darling had '[taken] the fight to Alex Salmond in terms that were often starkly personal', the *Times* columnist commented further, 'At times it seemed like a debate on Mr Salmond as much as the issue of independence'.[73] This approach by the leader of Better Together also drew critique, however, such as in the following submission to the *Herald*, which commented, 'from the beginning of the televised debate Alistair Darling turned the debate into a very personalised one, attacking Alex Salmond in his first statement', with the author finding the former Chancellor's performance to be 'very distasteful from a politician of Mr Darling's standing and a very poor message from Better Together'.[74]

All the same, the personalisation of the referendum debate around Alex Salmond continued to be emphasised throughout the period in question, to the point where it is an all but unavoidable feature of much of the discourse. Commenting in the aftermath of the second debate, the *Telegraph* would assert, 'The SNP is trying to make the contest near-presidential, and Mr Salmond is doing his best to cast himself as the embodiment of Scottish aspiration', in doing so citing the responsibility for this trend as laying with the First Minister and his party, apparently ignoring the degree to which the newspaper's own coverage often focused near-exclusively on the leader of the SNP.[75] This position would be challenged in a piece by Robbie Dinwoodie, who noted the attempts to distance Salmond from the idea of independence while remarking on the apparent failure to achieve such an aim: 'Despite attempts by some in the Yes camp to move the focus away from him, Mr Salmond has been seen as synonymous with the Scottish independence movement'.[76] Equating Salmond with the notion of independence remained a consistent feature of the coverage, with Scotland becoming its own state again being presented as a possibility or ideal intrinsically linked to the First Minister. 'If Scotland votes Yes today, it will be the realisation of a long-held dream by a steely and driven man who has always believed that Scotland should be independent', remarked Emma Cowing in the *Mail*, while a number of letters published in this period provided evidence to suggest that the personalisation of the independence debate around Alex Salmond had been in some way assimilated by parts of the electorate: 'Alex Salmond is drive by self-ego and not the facts. This referendum is about the future of Scotland, it is not about having Alex Salmond being President of a Republic of Scotland'.[77]

Alan Cochrane would note in his referendum diary that 'the biggest weakness in the Yes campaign was allowing itself to be totally dominated by Alex Salmond', arguably overlooking the fact that both the First Minister and the wider Yes campaign evidently had little influence over what was published by predominantly Unionist newspaper titles.[78] Certainly, the personalisation of the debate even occurred in those outlets which were less hostile to independence, as seen in the headline of a *Sun* editorial appearing on page one the day before the referendum: *BRITAIN'S GOT TALENT V THE ECKS FACTOR*.[79] Though on one level simply a pun which played on the names of two popular Saturday night television shows, the use of such language nonetheless subtly reinforced the idea that the choice for the electorate was between Alex Salmond and the United Kingdom. Of course, that this should have been the case may not be particularly surprising, given that Salmond was First Minister, leader of the SNP and the most high-profile and established voice in the Yes campaign. However, one can also speculate that such coverage was in some ways deliberate, with the more Unionist press perhaps understanding or believing that 'Alex Salmond's independence' was a less attractive option to undecided voters than the possibilities presented by a more abstract, depersonalised conceptualisation of Scotland becoming its own state.

Of course, this trend was both observed and commented upon during the referendum period itself, with this personalisation of the debate being challenged on occasion, particularly by commentators endorsing a Yes vote. 'The personalisation of the campaign, as if independence was just about Mr Salmond's vanity, is typical of much conventional journalism', argued Iain MacWhirter, a week after the first televised debate.[80] Lesley Riddoch also commented on this aspect of the referendum coverage, again stressing that the focus on Salmond resulted predominantly from editorial decisions within the media:

> [the] constructed image of the mighty First Minister has elements of truth but substantially more elements of media creation which have allowed the Yes campaign to be portrayed as nothing more than an empty vessel for the boundless ambition and crazy, separatist urges of Big Eck.

Riddoch would continue, drawing attention to the fact that, given the priorities and established practices of the newspaper industry, the framing of the referendum in such personalised terms was to be in some ways expected: 'in a political landscape so devoid of striking personalities it was inevitable that a man so capable in the limelight and so fond of it should prompt a spot of mythmaking by a wrong-footed and personality-focused media'.[81] Such an admission would even occasionally appear in those outlets which had been actively framing the debate in such terms, such as in a *Mail* editorial which argued, 'the vote is not some test of the popularity of Prime Minister David Cameron, nor is it about his party. It is not even, in truth, about Salmond and the Nationalists'.[82]

Challenging this dominant narrative, which equated the prospects of an independent Salmond explicitly and persistently with Alex Salmond, ultimately found the greatest expression in the letters pages of the newspapers cited. 'Much of the media's attention focuses on Alex Salmond himself', noted a submission to the *Express*, which further opined on how such constant attention had shaped and strengthened the First Minister: 'Taking so much flak from internal and external opponents over the years has caused him to toughen up, and a strong natural belief in Scottish independence continues to drive him'.[83] In another example, advocating for a Yes vote, a letter to the *Mail* would question: 'Do all those who will vote No in the referendum realise it is nothing to do with Mr Salmond or the SNP, but to give Scotland true democracy at last?'[84] Echoing such assertions, others highlighted the importance of the vote, emphasising that the decision was about much more than simply an individual or political party. 'However, like him or loathe him, Mr Salmond is not what voters should focus on next month', argued one such letter to the *Herald*, 'The referendum is not about any of the individuals now, having their hour upon the stage, but the governance of Scotland for all time coming'.[85] Such a position was repeated in the *Scotsman*, with the author of one letter asserting simply, 'We need to remember that we are voting for a vision of Scotland in 2024 and 2124, way post-Alex Salmond and David Cameron'.[86] Such interventions evidently had little impact on the overall coverage, however, with it remaining the case that, in general, press attention persistently framed Salmond as being synonymous with independence.

Notes

1 Gill, "Salmond's parting gift".
2 Emma Cowing, "The man utterly determined to shatter the United Kingdom", *Mail*, 18.9.14, p. 17.
3 Letts, "One deft flick".
4 Alex Massie, "Salmond can win but he will have to try something new to him – humble pie", *Mail*, 25.8.14, p. 14.
5 Frank White, "Not football, Alex", *Mail*, 24.9.14, p. 58.
6 Chris Deerin, "Hubris, delusions of grandeur, and why a TV flop may be Alex's Wizard of Oz moment", *Mail*, 11.8.14, p. 14.
7 Cochrane, "Keep saying it".
8 Alan Roden, "How Salmond 'lost the plot' in front of the world's media", *Mail*, 12.9.14, p. 5.
9 Alan Cochrane, "Salmond's all snarls as he shows us his true colours", *Telegraph*, 12.9.14, p. 8.
10 Alan Cochrane, "Ultimately, this debate boils down to a question of trust", *Telegraph*, 22.9.14, p. 13.
11 Andrew Nicoll, "Any answers after currency plan took a pounding", *Sun*, 11.8.14, p. 8.
12 Editorial, "Show us you're on the money, Eck", *Record*, 8.8.14, p. 6.
13 Leckie, "651 days on".
14 Editorial, "Fight to finish", *Sun*, 11.8.14, p. 8.
15 Simon Johnson & Ben Riley-Smith, "Salmond's leadership under fire after debate disaster", *Telegraph*, 7.8.14, p. 1.

16 Simon Johnson, "Senior nationalist has called off campaign mobs, says Murphy", *Telegraph*, 3.9.14, p. 7.
17 Hamish Macdonell & Lindsay McIntosh, "Salmond is accused of failing to halt 'mob'", *Times*, 1.9.14, p. 1.
18 Roger Cartwright, "Salmond dictating to foreign country", *Scotsman*, 14.8.14, p. 30.
19 Michael Deacon, "Salmond turns his back on the question of abuse", *Telegraph*, 18.9.14, p. 6.
20 Brian Monteith, "Blame for ugly scenes can be laid at Salmond's doorstep", *Scotsman*, 1.9.14, p. 24.
21 Jonathan Brocklebank, "A cyclical gambler who ran the race of his life... then fell at the last", *Mail*, 20.9.14, p. 4.
22 Harry Reid, "Whatever the result, we are all winners in this debate...", *Herald*, 2.9.14, p. 13.
23 Paul Gilbride, "'Dictator' Salmond dodges big questions", *Express*, 12.9.14, p. 5.
24 Gareth Rose, "Korea boost for SNP as Kim Jong-Un backs split", *Mail*, 17.9.14, p. 5.
25 Editorial, "A chilling glimpse of the future if Scots vote 'Yes'", *Express*, 12.9.14, p. 12.
26 Deerin, "Hubris, delusions of grandeur".
27 Editorial, "Salmond's stance will drag Scotland down", *Telegraph*, 11.9.14, p. 8.
28 Editorial, "Salmond's bizarre Mandela delusion".
29 Cowing, "The man utterly determined".
30 David Aaronovitch, "The glory of independence is just a mirage", *Times*, 7.8.14, p. 23.
31 Tom Peterkin, "Salmond orders his party: 'Go out and win'", *Scotsman*, 22.8.14, p. 1; Editorial, "If Salmond cannot win a Yes vote then SNP is lost", *Express*, 8.8.14, p. 12.
32 Deerin, "Hubris, delusions of grandeur".
33 David Clegg, "The poll star", *Record*. 2.9.14, p. 9; Letts, "The Salmondistas".
34 Archie MacPherson, "Don't let Salmond's loudmouths bully their way to independence", *Record*, 18.9.14, p. 6.
35 Letts, "The Salmondistas".
36 Magnus Linklater, "Writer criticises Yes camp 'thought police'", *Herald*, 17.9.14, p. 6.
37 Martin Redfern, "SNP's true colours", *Mail*, 24.9.14, p. 58.
38 Gill, "Salmond's parting gift".
39 Kathleen Leslie, "Orwell classic may give a vision of our future", *Express*, 17.9.14, p. 25.
40 Lindsay McIntosh, "Salmond the bruiser rallies to dominate final TV debate", *Times*, 26.8.14, p. 1.
41 Editorial, "Alex wins it on points".
42 Paul Gilbride, "Salmond falls on his sword", *Express*, 20.9.14, p. 1; Tom Peterkin, "Salmond to step down as First Minister after defeat in referendum", *Scotsman*, 20.9.14, p. 2.
43 David Clegg, "The dream shall never die", *Record*, 20.9.14, p. 1; "End of a dream", *Times*, 20.9.14, p. 1.
44 Magnus Gardham, "My time as leader is nearly over but for Scotland the dream shall never die", *Herald*, 20.9.14, p. 1.

45 Lindsay McIntosh et al., "Salmond quits as powers for Scotland are blocked", *Times*, 20.9.14, p. 1.
46 Gill, "Salmond's parting gift".
47 Letts, "One deft flick".
48 Magnus Linklater, "Love him or hate him, Salmond brought about a debate that Scotland had to have", *Times*, 20.9.14, p. 5.
49 Ian Bell, "A man who thought big for a small nation", *Herald*, 20.9.14, p. 2.
50 AM Smith, "We cannot trust Westminster", *Herald*, 11.9.14, p. 17.
51 David Torrance, "Political chameleon who made a Scottish state a possibility", *Times*, 20.9.14, p. 4; David Torrance, "Volcanic Alex made independence possible and leaves much for his successor to take on", *Scotsman*, 20.9.14, p. 3.
52 David Clegg, "We now have the opportunity to hold Westminster's feet to the fire on the vow they've made", *Record*, 20.9.14, p. 2.
53 Editorial, "Resignation words that throw down gauntlet to the Unionist parties", *Herald*, 20.9.14, p. 18; Andy Philip, "Changing the future of Britain...the enduring legacy of Alexander Elliott Salmond", *Record*, 20.9.14, p. 7.
54 Brocklebank, "A cynical gambler".
55 Editorial, "Dreamer, charmer and fighter...will we see his like again?", *Record*, 20.9.14, p. 10.
56 Linklater, "Love him or hate him".
57 Editorial, "Resignation words".
58 Philip, "Changing the future".
59 Editorial, "Dreamer, charmer and fighter".
60 Editorial, "True colossus", *Sun*, 20.9.14, p. 4.
61 Iain MacWhirter, "He likes to choose his moment. He wanted to go out if not on a high then at least with his head held high", *Herald*, 20.9.14, p. 3; Torrance, "Political chameleon".
62 Linklater, "Love him or hate him".
63 Letts, "One deft flick".
64 Editorial, "Salmond falls with a flurry of punches", *Mail*, 20.9.14, p. 18.
65 Dean Herbert, "Salmond's plan for indy 'coup'", *Express*, 22.9.14, p. 1; Alan Roden, "Salmond's sinister threat to ignore the vote", *Mail*, 22.9.14, p. 1.
66 Editorial, "Accept the result or go now, Mr Salmond", *Mail*, 24.9.14, p. 14.
67 Lesley Riddoch, "From leading his party to the brink of victory [...]", *Scotsman*, 20.9.14, p. 34.
68 Lesley Riddoch, "Seconds out for Round 2 of TV debate", *Scotsman*, 25.8.14, p. 23.
69 David Torrance, "From 'young Robespierre" to big beast, it is difficult to imagine politics without him", *Herald*, 20.9.14, p. 3.
70 Torrance, "Political chameleon".
71 Lindsay McIntosh & Sam Coates, "Victory in reach for Salmond, poll shows", *Times*, 2.9.14, p. 1.
72 Simon Johnson, "Salmond fails to find an answer", *Telegraph*, 6.8.14, p. 1; Editorial, "Dry Alistair".
73 Massie, "Rarely has Mr Salmond".
74 Catriona Clark, "Salmond won the plaudits, but he did not win the debate", *Herald*, 27.8.14, p. 14.
75 Editorial, "Hearts over minds", *Telegraph*, 27.8.14, p. 17.
76 Robbie Dinwoodie, "The gambler out of aces who knew when to fold", *Herald*, 20.9.14, p. 2.

77 Cowing, "The man utterly determined"; John Richardson, "Citizenship scandal", *Mail*, 6.8.14, p. 54.
78 Cochrane, *Alex Salmond*.
79 Editorial, "Britain's got talent v the Ecks factor", *Sun*, 17.8.14, p. 1.
80 MacWhirter, "Time to stop".
81 Riddoch, "Seconds out".
82 Editorial, "Labour's late show".
83 Ian Irving, "In-depth view reveals scope of Alex's talents", *Express*, 29.8.14, p. 50.
84 Douglas Gray, "Chance for real democracy", *Mail*, 13.8.4, p. 52.
85 Stephen Nisbet, "Positive case for voting No lies in being proud of what we have", *Herald*, 1.9.14, p. 14.
86 Graham Vokes, "Patriot games", *Scotsman*, 9.9.14, p. 26.

8 The same old script? Thoughts regarding the coverage

Evidently then, the press coverage of the 2014 Scottish independence referendum was dominated by two key themes: these being discussions surrounding issues of policy, and discourse surrounding the interventions of certain elite individuals. With regard to the evaluation and critique of policy issues, many of those central to the 2014 debate will no doubt retain a critical importance going forward as debates over Scottish independence continue in the years ahead. Currency arrangements in an independent Scotland will continue to generate a variety of claims, and wider economic issues may well prove of even greater significance to the electorate once the full financial impact of the coronavirus pandemic has been felt. Debates regarding oil are also likely to remain a persistent aspect of press engagement, though developing global concerns over the role of fossil fuels in climate change may see the nature and tone of such coverage prove slightly different from that observed in 2014.

A major focal point which will undoubtedly remain a central concern will be the NHS, which has gathered a level of press attention, as a result of Covid-19, unmatched for decades. Discussions of this national institution will thus no doubt inform several aspects of political campaigning should the issue of independence be once again placed in the hands of the Scottish electorate, and the respective performances of the Scottish and UK governments in responding to the ongoing health crisis may well prove among the most important issues in such a debate. Concerns related to defence and strategic policy will no doubt remain significant, though will be largely shaped by whatever contemporary issues dominate the news agenda at the time of a second vote. More significant changes may be observed regarding the issue of EU membership, given that Scotland voted to remain in 2016 and yet was forced to leave all the same.

DOI: 10.4324/9781003138259-8

The influence of personalities, demonstrably a major factor in the campaigning and coverage of the 2014 referendum, will no doubt persist, however the independence debate unfolds in the years to follow. Perhaps underlining the length of time since the historic vote, many of the individuals discussed in this book are no longer part of the political landscape. Gordon Brown and Alistair Darling have both moved on to pastures new, while David Cameron and Alex Salmond no longer hold political office. Indeed, an interesting problem arises in speculating on the potential leader of the Unionist campaign, in the event of a further referendum. Were it to happen in the next few years one could safely assume that Nicola Sturgeon would assume the leadership position within the official pro-independence campaign, but candidates for the opposite role are few and far between. Although it is conceivable that someone from the previous campaign could resume such a position, a more likely candidate may be Ruth Davidson, who has been framed by several sections of the media as something of a Unionist champion in the years following 2014. Even without being leader of her party at Holyrood, Davidson's political star and reputation remain far more established than any of her Scottish colleagues. Further, the possibility of her inclusion in a future independence campaign could well see a major shift from 2014, in that the coverage would be focused on two female politicians, a direct contrast with the largely male-centric debate of seven years ago.

Despite it being the case that the newspaper industry continues a trend of decline, it retains an important role in society and in the dissemination of political information. Though some aspects of the media came in for criticism for the manner in which the 2014 referendum was reported, one can make the credible argument that a second vote on the issue of independence could, at least temporarily, reinvigorate the print media. Indeed, depending on how they collectively provide news and opinion, it is not inconceivable that the press could salvage a reputation which has been tarnished by a variety of factors in recent decades. Providing a balanced, multifaceted and comprehensive treatment of the independence debate could well contribute to a reengagement with politics as seen in 2014, though it is of course likely that several titles will simply double-down on their coverage from before. Scotland's referendum may have changed the country, but whether it has changed the newspaper industry in any notable way remains to be seen.

The results of the 6 May 2021 Scottish election show that the independence question is likely to continue to anchor and shape Scottish politics for the foreseeable future. Amidst a record turnout of some

63.5% the SNP went on to secure a fourth successive victory in a Scottish parliamentary election, a notable achievement in itself. Though falling one short of the 65 required to secure an outright majority, the 8 seats won by the Scottish Greens ensures that there is once again a pro-independence majority in the Scottish Parliament. Though both Boris Johnson and Nicola Sturgeon have insisted that the handling of the coronavirus pandemic must take immediate precedence, Scottish independence seems destined to become a live issue in years to come. Should this be the case, it is an inevitability that Scotland's newspaper industry will remain an integral conduit for the dissemination of various political ideas, though whether the coverage will bear any resemblance to that observed in 2014 remains highly speculative. Many of the personalities highlighted in the independence referendum are no longer part of the political scene, while emerging and ongoing issues – both domestically and on the international stage – will undoubtedly shape the framing of any future campaign. Nonetheless, few of the titles (or individual contributors) have drastically altered their editorial stance on Scottish independence, and so many of the trends and observations discussed in these pages will likely remain central to any evolving or accelerating discourse regarding Scotland's constitutional future.

Index